COLLABORATIVE COGNITIVE-BEHAVIORAL INTERVENTION IN SOCIAL WORK PRACTICE

Collaborative Cognitive-Behavioral Intervention in Social Work Practice

A WORKBOOK

Jacqueline Corcoran, Ph.D.

OXFORD
UNIVERSITY PRESS

OXFORD
UNIVERSITY PRESS

Oxford University Press is a department of the University of Oxford.
It furthers the University's objective of excellence in research, scholarship,
and education by publishing worldwide.

Oxford   New York
Auckland   Cape Town   Dar es Salaam   Hong Kong   Karachi
Kuala Lumpur   Madrid   Melbourne   Mexico City   Nairobi
New Delhi   Shanghai   Taipei   Toronto

With offices in
Argentina   Austria   Brazil   Chile   Czech Republic   France   Greece
Guatemala   Hungary   Italy   Japan   Poland   Portugal   Singapore
South Korea   Switzerland   Thailand   Turkey   Ukraine   Vietnam

Oxford is a registered trademark of Oxford University Press
in the UK and certain other countries.

Published in the United States of America by
Oxford University Press
198 Madison Avenue, New York, NY 10016

Library of Congress Cataloging-in-Publication Data
Corcoran, Jacqueline.
Collaborative cognitive-behavioral intervention in social work practice : a workbook / Jacqueline Corcoran.
    pages cm
ISBN 978–0–19–993715–8 (pbk. : alk. paper)   1. Social service.   2. Social service—Practice.
3. Counselor and client.   4. Cognitive therapy.   I. Title.
HV40.C672 2014
361.3'2—dc23
2013044485

CONTENTS

SECTION FOUR SKILL-BUILDING

SECTION FIVE COLLABORATION

ACKNOWLEDGMENTS

This book was a complex, multi-faceted endeavor, and I had a lot of assistance along the way. Many thanks to Clara Shockley and Jessie Kadolph for their excellent formatting and Clara Shockley and Francesca Tiexeira for their preparation of the reference list. I also appreciate the following students for sharing their learning process in this book: Megan Adair-Casteel, Jody Baumstein, Amanda Brice, Meagan Bullock, Dave Connolly, Nathaniel Dressell, Gelila Habte, Amanda Harvey, Caroline Jones, Lisa Katerman, Ericka Olschewski, Anna Regan, Jessica Shaaf Rozzelle, Tommy Saunders, Amanda Stager, and Lauren Stewart.

SECTION ONE

INTRODUCTION
AND OVERVIEW

CHAPTER 1

INTRODUCTION AND OVERVIEW OF COGNITIVE-BEHAVIORAL INTERVENTION

The purpose of *Collaborative Cognitive-Behavioral Social Work Intervention: A Workbook* is to teach social work students behavioral and cognitive-behavioral techniques so that they are better able to help clients with problems of living. Cognitive-behavioral intervention involves a broad class of present-focused techniques that derive philosophically, theoretically, and empirically from four theories of learning (Macdonald, 2009): classical conditioning, operant conditioning, observational learning, and cognitive learning.

In this introductory chapter, a definition and overview of these theories is offered. Readers will see that there are many potential problems to which cognitive-behavioral therapy (CBT) can be applied, in the course of working with various clients during social work internship and employment. These problems include anger management, child behavior problems, substance use disorder, depression, and anxiety, among others. Although CBT will not solve every presenting problem—social workers will often want to target different systems levels—CBT is a goal-focused, present-oriented way to help clients at an individual level better cope with stressful life events and change behaviors that interfere with better adjustment to such events.

OVERVIEW

The earliest part of the theory behind CBT began with behaviorism, which became prominent in the social sciences during the first half of the twentieth century. Among its pioneers were Pavlov (1932, 1934), Watson (1930), and Skinner (1953). They developed theories of *conditioning*, which is the process of developing patterns of behavior through responses to environmental stimuli or specific behavioral consequences (Wilson, 2013). The earliest of these theories involved *classical conditioning*, in which an initially neutral stimulus (e.g., the bell) comes to produce a conditioned response (e.g., dog salivating) after being paired repeatedly with a conditioned stimulus (food) (Pavlov, 1932, 1934). Classical conditioning plays a role in the understanding of many behavioral problems that clients experience. For example, previously neutral cues, such as certain places (restaurants or bars, dorms), people (drinking buddies), or feeling states (i.e., boredom), may become associated with problem behaviors, such as overeating or substance use disorder. Many anxiety-related disorders are classically conditioned. Treatment of behavioral problems associated with classical conditioning is discussed in Chapter 2.

Another behavioral theory that developed was *operant conditioning*; its main premise is that future behavior is determined by the consequences of present behavior (Skinner, 1953). Positive reinforcement increases the behavior that precedes it. Negative reinforcement occurs when a person's behavior leads one to avoid, escape from, or stop experiencing an unpleasant event, making the behavior more likely to occur in the future. Alcohol use, for example, is negatively reinforcing if it leads to escape from uncomfortable or distressing feelings. Operant conditioning also involves extinction (or ignoring) and punishment, other events that follow behaviors. Chapter 3 delves into operant conditioning behavioral interventions, which have many applications in social work.

Modeling theory involves the vicarious learning that takes place when people observe others indulging in a particular behavior and see them being reinforced for it (Bandura, 1977). The observers are thus more likely to adopt the behavior themselves. Modeling is used not only to explain the acquisition of behaviors but also as one of the methods of delivery for cognitive-behavioral interventions (see Chapter 11).

Over time, cognitions (thoughts, beliefs) came to be seen as learned behaviors. The centrality of beliefs for feelings and behaviors was a focus of intervention (Beck, 2011). The process of cognitive restructuring was formulated from two different schools of cognitive therapy: rational-emotive therapy, by Ellis (Ellis & McLaren, 1998), and cognitive therapy, by Beck (Beck, 1976; Beck & Freeman, 1990). Chapter 5 covers the use of cognitive restructuring in social work.

SOCIAL WORK AND CBT

Other than the fact that CBT can be helpful for treating many client problems, there are additional reasons why learning cognitive-behavioral interventions is important for social workers.

EVIDENCE-BASED PRACTICE

First, *Collaborative Cognitive-Behavioral Social Work Intervention: A Workbook* reflects the movement in social work, as well as in other medical and social services fields, toward evidence-based practice. Increasingly, social workers are being held to standards of accountability that require them to use methods that have been supported by the best available evidence. The process of decision-making using evidence-based practice involves bringing the available evidence to bear on a particular practice model. An intervention is selected on the basis of the evidence itself; the practice context; the expertise of social workers and their values and ethics; and client characteristics, preferences, and motivation (Sackett, Richardson, Rosenberg, & Haynes, 1997). Social workers have a responsibility to their clients to intervene with the most effective theoretical methods possible—methods that have been tested and that have proven clinical utility.

In reviews involving various problem areas, CBT has been found to have disproportionate success as a researched treatment (Chambless & Hollon, 1998; Corcoran, 2011). Table 1.1 shows the problem areas for which CBT has emerged with empirical support; others are detailed in Appendices A and B.

Unfortunately, social work lags behind other mental health professions in terms of graduate level training in cognitive-behavioral intervention. Weissman, Verdeli, and colleagues (2006) surveyed training directors of psychiatry, psychology, and social work programs in the United States to determine the extent of "gold standard training" present in graduate school education for those interventions that had empirical support. "Gold standard training" was defined as both a didactic course and supervised clinical work in an empirically supported treatment model. The two disciplines with the largest number of students training primarily for clinical practice, the PsyD and the MSW, required the lowest percentage of gold standard training. Social work faculty explained the lack of coursework and clinical supervision for empirically supported treatments by the fact that their mandate was not to provide training in psychotherapy. Indeed, the mission of social work is to bring services and resources to oppressed and vulnerable populations, to improve their quality of life and bring about social economic and justice (National Association of Social Workers [NASW], 1997). In this book, however, the argument is made that cognitive-behavioral interventions do not need to be limited to psychotherapy uses, even though social workers are indeed the largest providers of psychotherapy in the United States (Weissman, Wickramaratne, et al., 2006). Social workers are employed in a diversity of settings—child welfare, family support programs, hospitals, schools, clubhouses for people with mental illness, programs for individuals with intellectual disabilities, long-term care facilities, hospice—and there are many

TABLE 1.1: **Studies on CBT**

Topics	Studies
Pain and health management	Bernardy, Fuber, Kollner, & Hauser, 2010; Dissanyake & Bertouch, 2010; Fors, Bertheussen, Thune, et al., 2010; Thomas, Thomas, Hillier, et al., 2006
Anxiety	Hofmann & Smits, 2008; James, Soler, & Weatherall, 2005; Macdonald, Higgins, & Ramchandani, 2006
Borderline personality disorder	Kliem, Kröger, & Kosfelder, 2010; Lynch, Chapman, & Rosenthal, 2006
Anger, defiance, and aggression	Armelius & Andreassen, 2007; Lipsey, Landenberger, & Wilson, 2007; Mytton, Diguiseppi, Gough, Taylor, & Logan et al., 2006; Wilson & Lipsey, 2006a, 2006b

more. Cognitive-behavioral interventions have been developed to target a number of problems that may arise in these contexts, such as child behavior problems, anger management, family conflict, and those that develop as a result of accumulated life stressors.

SOCIAL WORK VALUES AND CBT

Another reason for learning CBT is that it shares certain values of social work. The importance of the environment is one of these values, although CBT defines *environment* as an immediate system, such as a classroom, other group, or family, that acts to control the contingencies of a person's behavior. A behavioral assessment that takes into account the biological, psychological, and social cues is also compatible with the biopsychosocial perspective in social work, although the environment considered in social work extends far beyond the immediate context, such as culture, the political economy, and other encompassing social structures.

Social work prides itself on having a holistic, strengths-based perspective. A major, implied strength of CBT is the principle of learning: if a behavior was once learned, it can be unlearned and replaced with more functional patterns. In other words, the person is not inherently flawed. CBT is generally averse to the use of labels and generalizations. When it comes to change efforts, talking with labels limits our understanding of the specific nature of the problem. It also implicitly sets up an expectation that the person or the situations will always remain the same, that we are referring to immutable traits and situations. In contrast, talking about concrete manifestations of behavior is usually less pathologizing; it also creates more optimism about the possibility of change. After all, changing entrenched personality traits might be next to impossible, but we may be able to help a person change specific behaviors, such as complying rather than yelling when a girl's mother tells her to do a chore.

Certain misconceptions abound about CBT interventions, including that they "are disempowering, dehumanizing, mechanical, rely on aversive control...only address superficial problems, ignore the importance of the therapeutic relationships, and teach people to manipulate each other" (Bach & McCracken, n.d.). However, when applied properly, CBT can be an empowering approach to change, helping clients learn how to take control of their actions and their immediate environment through learning new skills and ideas. The emphasis in this book will be on the importance of relationship factors—empathy, warmth, and a generally caring attitude—as they are vitally important to clients, perhaps more than the methods that are used (Karver, Handelsman, & Fields, 2006; Wampold, 2011). It is also important to know how to deliver CBT in a way that is respectful of client circumstances and works with clients collaboratively.

FORMAT

Collaborative Cognitive-Behavioral Social Work Intervention: A Workbook presents knowledge about behavioral and cognitive interventions in an easy-to-read, jargon-free manner.

In this volume, I have culled CBT to its essentials, so that readers will not get unnecessarily bogged down in theory and details. Abundant examples are offered, to enable readers to see the diverse range of applications that cognitive-behavioral interventions might have to social work.

Readers' grasp of content, as well as its application, is developed and tested through multiple-choice and short-answer quizzes. Instructors can use these as in-class exercises or as homework. A companion website is available to provide the answers.

One of the main advantages of this workbook, other than its emphasis on *how to do CBT*, is to show its relevance to populations and problems beyond the private practice and university settings with which CBT has been traditionally associated. Many books on CBT have emerged from the field of psychology and discuss clients from middle- or upper-class backgrounds. This book reflects social work's commitment to bringing services to people who are impoverished and oppressed. The step-by-step delivery of CBT in a respectful and collaborative manner, with regard for the realistic context of the client's life, is an emphasis of this book.

The first sections of the book cover the building blocks of the CBT model—operant conditioning, respondent conditioning, cognitive interventions, and skill-building. Using the examples and exercises, students will understand the "common elements" of CBT practice (Chorpita, Becker, & Daleiden, 2007) that cross-cut the treatment manuals described in the appendices offered at the end of the book. The interested reader is encouraged to seek out manuals that address the specific problem for which a particular client is being seen.

Although the examples and exercises throughout the book show how CBT can be delivered in a collaborative fashion with understanding of the reality of the client's circumstances, the last section of the book focuses more specifically on collaboration. This section covers timing of CBT interventions according to client readiness and how to build motivation to change. It is also intended to help social workers provide information in a way that clients can receive and explore, without invoking defensiveness. Other methods of delivery are also covered, such as the importance of role-plays and homework to enhance generalizability of skills, so that clients are better positioned to meet their life goals.

SECTION TWO
BEHAVIORAL MODELS

CHAPTER 2

CLASSICAL CONDITIONING

The book starts with classical conditioning, as it is the earliest formulation of behaviorism. From your undergraduate psychology classes, you are likely already familiar with Pavlov's research, which is briefly reviewed in this chapter. Despite the fact that classical conditioning was first conceptualized in the 1930s, the elements of classical conditioning are still relevant today because they play a role in the development of many behavioral and emotional problems that clients experience.

PAVLOV'S RESEARCH

In Pavlov's (1932) famous research with dogs, food naturally produced salivation in dogs. The food, therefore, was the conditioned stimulus. A bell rung at the same time as the presentation of the food initially failed to evoke salivation. However, after the bell was paired with food repeatedly, the bell in itself started to evoke salivation in the dogs. The bell at this point attained the status of a conditioned stimulus, as it was capable of producing a response.

The discovery of these principles has important implications for many problem behaviors that people develop. They start to associate (in other words, they are conditioned by) certain internal cues (feelings or thoughts) and external events and people, places, and things with a particular behavior. See Example 2.1.

EXAMPLE 2.1: CLASSICAL CONDITIONING

1. A person who smokes marijuana to deal with depression may start to associate the mood state of depression with smoking marijuana.

2. A stressful experience of giving a presentation in front of a group of people might generalize to a fear of all public presentations.

3. If a person binge drinks with certain friends, then when she sees those friends, she may have the urge to drink.

Because respondent conditioning is a powerful way that behavioral patterns develop over time, the social worker, as part of a biopsychosocial assessment, can ask clients about the cues (also called *antecedents, stimulus conditions*, or *triggers*; these terms will be used interchangeably) that encourage certain behaviors.[1]

BIOLOGICAL CUES

Many cues are experienced at the biological or physical level. These include tension, pain, cravings for drugs, inattentiveness, and other sensations.

As an example, people addicted to opioids might have physical complaints, such as back pain, that trigger their use of substances initially. Over time, pain may act as a cue to take the drug to relieve the pain. Some drugs, such as opioids, barbiturates, and alcohol, can become physically addictive, and cravings may act as a strong motivator for continued abuse.

Alternatively, tension in the body from stress may cause a person who compulsively picks at her skin until it raises welts to continue to do this until she relaxes. In a person with an eating disorder, feeling too full may trigger purging. Restraint from eating over a long period of time can inevitably lead to overeating, as people give in to the biological necessity to eat and then go overboard.

Alcoholics Anonymous attendees are warned against becoming "too tired or hungry," as these are physical states that might make one susceptible to drinking. People who struggle with their weight are told to refrain from grocery shopping when they are hungry, as they may succumb to the temptation to buy all manner of fattening foods.

Questions for getting at physiological cues include the following (Cormier, Nurius, & Osborn, 2009, p. 204):

"Notice what goes on inside you just before this happens."
"Is there anything going on with you physically—an illness or physical condition—or anything about the way you eat, smoke, exercise, and so on, that affects or leads to this issue?"

PSYCHOLOGICAL CUES

The psychological aspect of the biopsychosocial assessment of triggers involves both thinking patterns and feelings.

---

1 Although a functional assessment from behavior therapy is often conceptualized as an ABC model (**A**ntecedents, the **B**ehavior that follows, and the **C**onsequences), this is suggested as a simpler model that can still lead to successful client work. The "behavior" here is an entrenched, patterned response that is generally consistent across time. Additionally, and in line with the topic of this chapter, the assessment at this point covers only those cues that have become classically reinforced.

THINKING PATTERNS

Cognitive-behavioral theorists believe that thoughts, attitudes, and beliefs (in other words, the things we tell ourselves) fuel our problem behaviors. For example, thinking "Nothing's going to turn out right," "This always happens," or "There's no hope" could start off a depressive cycle. Chapter 5 is devoted to identifying and changing problematic cognitions such as these.

FEELINGS

Although behavioral approaches tend to de-emphasize feelings, discussion of client's feelings is very important. First, conveying understanding of the client's feelings can help build the supportive alliance that is necessary for change to occur. Second, feelings are often triggers for problem behaviors. For instance, a person who is scared and may decide to threaten others in order to feel safer; a person who is bored may be more prone to using drugs. However, people are often unaware of the feelings that trigger them to act in certain ways. Therefore, building people's insight into their feelings and the behaviors they use to manage the feelings can provide them with information that is vital to their change efforts.

Some clients are aware of their feelings and will describe them; others will provide information perhaps nonverbally or more indirectly, and the social worker can infer the presence of a certain feeling. For example, a client's tearing up and having difficulty speaking obviously indicates sadness and can be reflected back to the client: ("You seem to be feeling really sad right now.")

Other people do not have a vocabulary for their emotions, or confuse what they think from what they feel. Some of the work in these cases involves helping people to distinguish the two, since thoughts are believed to influence feelings in CBT. Creed, Reisweber, and Beck (2011) suggest the following explanation: "Thoughts are in your head and are usually many words, and emotions are in your body, and they are usually described with one word. Thoughts can also be described as what you are saying to yourself, while emotions are what you feel inside." Another way to help clients differentiate between thoughts and feelings is to relabel them (Beck, 2005), as in Example 2.2.

EXAMPLE 2.2: DIFFERENTIATING THOUGHTS AND FEELINGS

Client: I feel like, why should I try to do anything new? They never appreciate it, and I didn't ask for this. They should be the ones to make some changes. It's so unfair!

Social Worker: And when you have those thoughts, "I shouldn't have to do anything new. They should be the ones to do this. It's unfair," how do you feel emotionally?

Client: I feel so mad!

Techniques for Teaching Children about Feelings

Play a game of charades in which children select feeling words and have to act them out. Have children go through magazines, cut out pictures of people having different feelings, and then paste them on a sheet of paper, labeling each one.

Trace a body-sized outline of the child and have the child color in different feelings where they are experienced in the body and label them, or have the child draw a picture of her- or himself and do a similar exercise.

Source: Podell, Martin, & Kendall (2009)

For sources where one can download a list of feelings to show clients, see websites such as http://www.psychpage.com/learning/library/assess/feelings.html, and http://childrenscenter.sa.ucsb.edu/CMSMedia/Documents/ParentSupport/FeelingWords. As these lists demonstrate, there are many nuanced words for different feelings, but the basic four are as follows:

- Anger
- Sadness
- Fear
- Happiness

All other feelings are variations of these. Anger encompasses frustration, irritation, annoyance, and rage, among other nuances. Sadness comprises hurt, as well as grief and loss. Fear encapsulates anxiety, nervousness, and embarrassment. Happiness involves contentment and pleasure, as well as ecstasy. Therefore, asking people to describe how they are feeling in these terms is sufficient.

Children may need assistance in developing a vocabulary for awareness and expression of feelings. Suggestions are offered in Table 2.1, with an application in Example 2.3.

EXAMPLE 2.3: TEACHING CHILDREN ABOUT FEELINGS

A social work intern was seeing David, age 11, an African-American male, who had been emotionally and physically abused by an uncle while his mother was in treatment for a 20-year addiction to heroin. He was told to write down as many feelings as he was aware of and then give an example of each, as well as the accompanying physical signs.

Feeling	Description of Circumstances	Physical Signs
Sad	"When no one in my family is around"	A hole in my chest
Mad	"When my brother messes with me"	Fists ball, head feels hot
Scared	"When my uncle was around"	Heart races
Happy	"When I'm with my sister and her baby"	Smiling

Note that children are taught to identify the sensations in their body that are associated with various emotions. This process can also be helpful for adults, as so many emotions are experienced as physical rather than emotional states. This tendency may be attenuated in people from some minority cultural groups, who sometimes experience emotional distress in terms of physical symptoms (U.S. Department of Health and Human Services, 2001).

SOCIAL CUES

The social aspect of the problem may involve both interactions with other people and the environment in which the behavior occurs, such as the neighborhood context. For example, depression or anger may be triggered by social events, which include rudeness, exploitation, or exclusion. If a person lives in a high-crime neighborhood with easy access to drugs, that may present a problem for those trying to get over an addiction. Being in a certain work environment that encourages drinking, such as restaurants or bars, may present risk for a person with a drinking problem. Living in a cramped and unsafe residence may make a person feel more stressed and vulnerable to abusing her children.

To conclude this discussion about, Exercise 2.1 asks you to identify the cues for a client's behavior at the biopsychosocial levels (Example 2.4).

EXAMPLE 2.4: HELPING BUILD CLIENTS' AWARENESS OF CUES: ANGER MANAGEMENT

A social work intern educated participants in an anger management group on the recognition of cues in the "escalation phase" of their anger. The focus here is on Edwin, a 45-year-old African-American man.

Edwin: Honestly, my problem is that I can't tell when my anger is escalating. I don't get angry that often, but when I do, I just explode in anger.

Social Work Intern: I see. So because you aren't able to recognize when your anger is escalating, you have a hard time controlling the angry outbursts.

Edwin: It's more than that. Sometimes when I meet people, I get a bad first impression. That's when I decide I don't like them. Then, if they cross me, I explode.

Social Work Intern: What are some of the things that can give you a bad first impression of someone?

Edwin: I can't really explain it. All I can say is that it doesn't happen that much anymore. I did get in trouble with the law over the summer, though, because of my anger, and I have a court date coming up.

(continued)

Social Work Intern: It sounds like it may not happen as much anymore, but it still has a negative effect on your life.

Edwin: Well, I ran into this guy on the street and I started talking to him. He started to get condescending and got all up in my face. I felt a little threatened, and I guess things escalated from there because we ended up getting into a fist fight. Now I gotta see what happens at this court date because he pressed charges against me.

Social Work Intern: You indicated that your anger was hard to control because you couldn't identify when it was escalating. Do you think that getting a bad first impression of someone could be part of your escalation phase?

Edwin: Well, when I started talking to this guy, things escalated quickly because I didn't like him. So I guess you have a point.

Social Work Intern: Everyone's escalation phase will look different, but this might be how you can start to recognize yours.

Edwin: Yea, I can see how this could be a sign of me losing control of anger.

EXERCISE 2.1: IDENTIFYING BIOPSYCHOSOCIAL TRIGGERS

Exercise Instructions: Pick a client and a specific problem behavior for the client. Identify the cues operating at each of the following levels.

Behavior:	
Biopsychosocial Levels	**Your Client Cues**
Biological	
Psychological	
Cognitive	
Emotional	
Social	
Relationships	
Environment/Context	

BEHAVIORAL CHAINS

Many people, such as Edwin in Example 2.4, view their problems as "coming out of the blue" or "just happening." They will make statements, such as, "Suddenly, I just snap and start screaming" or "I felt like having a drink, so I had one." However, it is more accurate to understand that sequences of events lead up to problem behaviors. For example, a person who says that she just "snapped" and hit her child with a belt leaving marks may have been stressed by a number of events that occurred that day, and the frustration and tension was building over several hours' time to culminate in an incident of abuse.

It is important for people to understand the chain of events and reactions that led up to the loss of control over their behavior. In that way, they can intervene at an earlier point and prevent its occurrence. Guidelines are provided here for helping clients construct a behavior chain, which involves a detailed examination of a serious, harmful behavior (e.g., physical violence, cutting, a suicide attempt, or a substance use disorder relapse) in terms of the sequences that are linked together by learned cues.

1. *Before* any incident occurs, prepare the client that a consequence of such a behavior will be to spend an in-depth analysis on it, figuring out exactly how this occurred and what can be done differently next time. See Table 2.2.
2. Maintain a supportive and empathic stance throughout.
3. Start at the beginning of the day, if necessary, if people have a hard time identifying the first step in the chain that led up to the behavior.
4. At each juncture, ask questions pertaining to the bio-psycho-social nature of the person:
   How did you feel physically? What was going on with you physically?
   (The client may reveal, for instance, that she had not slept well the night before, or that he was hung over from substance use from the night before, or hungry.)
   What were you feeling? How intense was the feeling? (1–10)
   What was going through your mind? What were you thinking?
   What event happened? Who was there? What did they say?
5. Recognize that people will most often start with the event that happened rather than their internal states: "My alarm didn't go off, and I was late. My children were sick, and I had to stay home and take care of them. I was fired." Then it will be necessary for you to probe for the nature of and the intensity of the thoughts and feelings.

TABLE 2.2: **Sample Rationale Dialogue**

Client: I just did it. It came out of the blue. It just happened. There is no reason.
Social Worker: I know it feels like this just comes out of the blue, but it actually might be helpful to know there are certain things that have built up to get you to this point. The fact that there are many factors involved for us to figure out means that there are also many things you can do in the future that will stop you from getting to this point. This will come easier to you as you develop more understanding of your triggers.

---

6. Record each of the sequences that you discuss. Linehan (1993) talks about index cards to track these sequences. To keep with the biopsychosocial framework of assessment you could use a template such as the following:

Sequence #1:		
Biological	Psychological	Social
Sequence #2		
Biological	Psychological	Social
Sequence #3		
Biological	Psychological	Social

7. If the client stalls, unable to remember or identify a cue, there are several options:
   - Say, "I know you don't know, so just make it up." This sometimes acts to allow clients to bypass the resistance of feeling as if they have to provide the "right" answer or being put on the spot.
   - Ask, "What would [your parent, child, boss, or another person intimately involved with the problem] say happened or how you might have been feeling?"
     Sometimes it's easier to answer questions from the perspective of another person.
   - Go to the next sequence that the person does remember.
   - Go backward from the incident itself.
   - If people minimize what happened or don't want to center on the discussion, repeat the rationale for this exercise (Table 2.3):
8. Once all the sequences have been identified, discuss each of the biopsychosocial spiritual aspects in terms of what could be done next time to prevent the behavior ultimately culminating (Example 2.5). (This is the topic of Chapter 8.)

(This example will be taken back up again in Chapter 8, when the development of coping plans is discussed.)

CLINICAL INTERVENTION

Intervention based on classical conditioning involves reversing the ways in which cues and behaviors became associated and breaking the connection between the two. Here the

---

TABLE 2.3: Sample Dialogue

Client: There were other things I wanted to talk to you about today. I don't want to spend all our time on this.
Social Worker: Remember when we first started, we talked about the fact that if there were any such incidents, then we would have to talk about them in detail so we can make sure that we can figure out what to do in the future to prevent these.

EXAMPLE 2.5: EXPLORING BEHAVIOR CHAINS

In the following example of Taryn, a 26-year-old white female who is seeing a social worker for a "cutting" problem, you will see how the social worker explores an incident of the behavior, tracking the events that happened over the course of that day to lead up to the cutting.

Social Worker: I know that we have been tracking the times that you cut yourself and you had indicated that it happened on Monday this past week. Let's start with that today.

Taryn: Do we have to? I have so much other stuff to talk about today.

Social Worker: I know, and I want to hear about it. However, we had agreed that it is really important to look at not using cutting as a way to cope with things. Let's walk through a behavioral analysis so we can figure out what other skills you can use in the future, and then we will get right down to the other things you have for today.

Taryn: All right.

Social Worker: So it looks like this happened on Monday. What was going on?

Taryn: I don't know. It's just like every other time. I just lose it and the next thing I know I'm in my bedroom cutting again.

Social Worker: Okay, let's try to re-create a chain of events for that day. Where should we start?

Taryn: Well, I cut Monday night.

Social Worker: That's fine. We can start there. Now, when did you have the first urge to cut?

Taryn: It just kinda came out of nowhere, like usual.

Social Worker: Did you wake up feeling that way?

Taryn: No, my day was going fine in the morning.

Social Worker: When did things start to turn bad?

Taryn: I guess it was when I looked through my mail. I had applied for a grant to help with my bills, and it was denied.

Social Worker: And was this when you first started thinking of cutting?

Taryn: No, I was really upset, but I had other stuff to do. But I did keep thinking about it throughout the day.

Social Worker: And what did you do after that?

Taryn: I had to run some errands and then went to visit my boyfriend, Chris. He is in jail right now and I can only go on Tuesdays at noon to see him.

Social Worker: How were you doing when you were running your errands?

Taryn: I guess I felt all right.

Social Worker: What about when you went to see Chris?

(continued)

Taryn: Well, that started okay, but it went downhill fast.

Social Worker: Can you tell me a little more?

Taryn: Yeah, I had to check in and wait quite awhile, but that is normal. I just spent the time texting a couple friends. When I finally got back to see him I was really excited. The minute I sat down though, I knew it wasn't gonna be a good visit. The first thing he asked was if I had brought money for his commissary account. I didn't have any extra money this week so I told him no. Then he just started yelling that I don't really care about him and that I shouldn't have even bothered coming.

Social Worker: What thoughts or feelings did that trigger for you?

Taryn: I was ticked off! I had to find someone to watch my daughter AND reschedule an appointment I had made just so I could come see him. I was also really hurt, too.

Social Worker: Any specific thoughts?

Taryn: Just that he doesn't care about me, he just wants money.

Social Worker: What happened next?

Taryn: Since I was already there I tried to change the conversation, but he kept bringing it up, so the rest of the visit was miserable.

Social Worker: What did you do after the visit?

Taryn: I went home after that. I had a little bit of time before I had to pick my daughter up from my mom's, and I was really upset and just wanted to be alone.

Social Worker: Were you thinking about cutting when you left the jail?

Taryn: Not yet, I was just so mad.

Social Worker: What happened when you got home?

Taryn: I just went into my bedroom and started crying. I couldn't stop thinking about how he treated me. Eventually I started to think, why do I even bother?

Social Worker: Is this when you cut?

Taryn: Yes, I was just feeling so overwhelmed.

Social Worker: What happened afterward?

Taryn: I felt a little more in control. I could at least stop crying.

Social Worker: Was that all?

Taryn: No, after a few minutes I started to feel guilty. My mom knows I cut and I recently promised her I would try to stop—she knows I see you, too, and that we are working on it. I knew I was going to have to go see her soon and pick up my daughter. Then I started thinking about not being a good mom to my daughter, because I turn to cutting all the time.

Social Worker: It really sounds like this turned out to be an incredibly tough day. Let's figure out what could be changed so that you don't feel you have to resort to cutting if you feel overwhelmed again.

Taryn: Yeah, I suppose we should spend some time on that.

TABLE 2.4: Methods of Exposure*

Type	Description
Imaginal	The client imagines that he or she is experiencing the situation or stimulus.
Interoceptive	The client is trained to mimic bodily reactions that arouse panic, such as exercise to speed up the heart rate or spinning in a chair to induce dizziness, and develop tolerance to them.
Simulated	Role-playing to invoke the situation.
In vivo	The client has contact with the real situation or stimulus.
Symbolic	Pictures or drawings of the feared object. For children, the practitioner can act out the situation using a puppet facing a feared object.

*Knell & Dasari (2009)

focus is on exposure, a technique that was developed to treat anxiety disorders (e.g., social anxiety, panic disorder, post-traumatic stress disorder), the focus of behavioral researchers initially (Wolpe, 1958). *Exposure* involves exposing people to what they fear until the anxiety response dissipates. There are a variety of methods to deliver exposure, as outlined in Table 2.4.

Because people have a hard time facing their fears rather than avoiding them, first they are taught how to relax on cue. Relaxation in this book is discussed under coping skills, the subject of Chapter 7. Clients should be practiced at being able to relax before they start facing their fears through exposure.

To keep people from feeling too overwhelmed, the next phase typically is to develop a fear hierarchy or ladder, which is a hierarchy of feared situations, from least to most feared. Deblinger and Heflin (1996, p. 74), in their treatment manual for child sexual abuse, list the memories of sexual abuse that children usually avoid. Their sample fear hierarchy is listed in Table 2.5.

After developing a list, the typical procedure is to work through the items in that order, conquering smaller fears before going on to tackle bigger ones. Clients learn to face each event or item on the list, starting with the least anxiety provoking, by learning to pair relaxation exercises with the event, rather than anxiety. In this process of systematic desensitization (Wolpe, 1958) people work their way through the rank ordering of fears until they are no longer plagued by the anxiety.

TABLE 2.5: Sample Fear Hierarchy: Child Sexual Abuse

1. General information about sexual abuse
2. Nonabusive interactions with the offender
3. The disclosure and resulting investigation
4. The first episode of abuse
5. Additional types of abusive contacts
6. Other specific episodes of abuse associated with major holidays, other anniversary dates
7. The most disturbing or embarrassing abusive episodes

CONCLUSION

As you have seen by the content of this chapter, classical conditioning, despite being conceptualized many years ago, has much relevance in today's social work practice. Many problem behaviors, such as substance use disorders and anxiety disorders and self-mutilating behaviors, have been classically conditioned. Understanding these behavioral patterns is important, as you can then help clients break these associations through relaxation and other techniques, which are the focus of Section 4.

TEST YOUR SKILLS EXERCISE 2.1: CLASSICAL CONDITIONING

Exercise Instructions: Circle the correct answer to each of the following questions.

1. Which of the following is NOT an example of classical conditioning:
   a. Each time you go into the kitchen you feel hungry.
   b. A child is put in timeout when they exhibit bad behavior.
   c. You get very sick after eating a dish with chicken in it. After this, even the smell of chicken begins to make you feel sick.
   d. You always take naps on the couch. Soon you begin to feel tired every time you sit on the couch.

2. Which of the following is the best beginning of a hierarchy for an exposure intervention:
   a. Pam has agoraphobia and can't leave the house. This will be the item that we begin working on in Pam's hierarchy.
   b. Devon has a fear of flying, so for his fear hierarchy he is working on developing alternate methods of transportation for travel needs.
   c. Reginald has a fear of germ contamination. His fear hierarchy starts with touching a door handle without washing his hands, the least fear-producing thing he could think of.
   d. Janice has a fear of speaking in front of others. Her fear hierarchy will start with giving a major presentation at work.

3. Intervention based on respondent conditioning involves the following EXCEPT:
   a. Learning to manage anxiety so that it is not overwhelming
   b. Avoiding cues that make one anxious
   c. Exposure to cues
   d. Breathing and relaxation training

4. In this case, the social work intern talked with Edwin, a 45-year-old African-American man, about his cues for anger. The questions below will ask you to analyze the exchange in terms of its collaborative nature.

(continued)

Edwin: Honestly, my problem is that I can't tell when my anger is escalating. I don't get angry that often, but when I do I just explode in anger.

Social Work Intern: I see. So because you aren't able to recognize when your anger is escalating, you have a hard time controlling angry outbursts.

Edwin: It's more than that. Sometimes when I meet people, I get a bad first impression. That's when I decide I don't like them. Then if they cross me, I go right to the explosion phase.

Social Work Intern: What are some of the things that can give you a bad first impression?

Edwin: Well, I ran into this guy on the street and I started talking to him. He started to get condescending and got all up in my face. I felt a little threatened and I guess things escalated from there because we ended up getting into a fist fight. Now I gotta see what happens at this court date because he pressed charges against me.

Social Work Intern: You indicated your anger was hard to control because you couldn't identify when it was escalating. Do you think that getting a bad first impression of someone could be part of your escalation phase?

Edwin: Well, when I started talking to this guy, things escalated quickly because I didn't like him. So I guess you have a point.

Social Work Intern: Everyone's escalation phase will look different, but this might be how you can start to recognize yours.

Edwin: Yeah, I can see how this could be a sign of me losing control of anger. You know, I really like these three stages because they make me think of things that I never pieced together before. Like how having to do time or show up for court is the post-explosion phase.

Social Work Intern: Right, because it happens as a consequence of your aggression in the explosion phase.

Edwin: Yeah.

Is this a good example of a collaborative intervention or not?

Explain specifically what was done to deliver information collaboratively.

CHAPTER 3

OPERANT CONDITIONING

This chapter will cover *operant conditioning*, the term referring to the class of techniques associated with reinforcement. The main premise of operant conditioning is that future behavior is determined by the consequences of present behavior (Skinner, 1953). The building blocks of operant conditioning are based on both positive and negative reinforcement. These are explained below with lots of practice examples and exercises. The key point to remember is that both types of reinforcement encourage behavior.

SOCIAL WORK APPLICATIONS

Interventions involving operant conditioning can be directly applied by social workers in settings where they have control over reinforcement, such as the following:

- Schools
- Hospitals
- Residential and group home treatment facilities
- Shelters

One of the more common uses for social workers of operant conditioning is when teaching parents discipline techniques to apply to their children's undesirable behaviors (referred to as *parent training*). There are many other problems, as well, for which operant conditioning is helpful (see Table 3.1).

REINFORCEMENT

Positive reinforcement is an event that increases the behavior preceding it. See Example 3.1. for examples of positive reinforcement.

Problem	Definition
Parent training	Teaching parents how to discipline their children using operant conditioning techniques
Community reinforcement training for substance use disorders	Providing reinforcement through tokens and rewards through gift cards and movie tickets for abstinence-related behavior
Behavior activation therapy for depression	Helping provide structure through daily scheduling and pleasurable activities to increase positive reinforcement and decrease negative reinforcement (social withdrawal)
Pervasive developmental disorders, applied behavior analysis (ABA) training	Defining discrete behaviors, reinforcing desirable behaviors, and ignoring or punishing undesirable behaviors
Alzheimer's disease	Clarifying target behaviors (e.g., bathing) and breaking them down into steps; identifying the relevant antecedent and consequent reinforcers of the target behavior, including the roles of significant others; and then enlisting caregivers to develop environmental conditions that will make the client more likely to exhibit the desired behavior

EXAMPLE 3.1: WAYS IN WHICH POSITIVE REINFORCEMENT INCREASES THE LIKELIHOOD OF A PROBLEM BEHAVIOR

Alcohol use is positively reinforced by the resultant feelings of well-being and pleasant social interaction with others.

A child's disruptive behavior in class may be reinforced if other children find it funny.

A father positively reinforces a child's talking back by giving him attention for it but he ignores the child when the he acts well.

Negative reinforcement is the process by which an unpleasant event is terminated by the individual's behavior. In this way, the particular behavior is reinforced. Examples follow in Example 3.2 and in Exercise 3.1 you can practice identifying reinforcement.

People often find the concept of negative reinforcement difficult to grasp. A common stumbling block seems to be the word *negative,* which people often translate to mean a "negative consequence," but that is punishment rather than reinforcement. The word *reinforcement* should be the salient one; remember that the definition of reinforcement is an event that follows a behavior that increases the behavior. Instead, apply the word *negative*

EXAMPLE 3.2: WAYS IN WHICH NEGATIVE REINFORCEMENT CAN CAUSE OR MAINTAIN PROBLEM BEHAVIORS

Alcohol use is negatively reinforcing if it leads to escape from uncomfortable or distressing feelings.

A parent's yelling is negatively reinforced if it results in even temporary child compliance with directions.

Avoidance from anxiety-provoking activities is negatively reinforced if it leads to anxiety being dissipated.

A man hits his partner to reduce his feelings of tension.

EXERCISE 3.1: IDENTIFYING POSITIVE AND NEGATIVE REINFORCEMENT

Exercise Instructions: In the following brief scenario, indicate where positive and negative reinforcement is taking place, and explain which behaviors are being reinforced.

A mother has imposed upon her 9-year-old son that he must complete homework before going outside to play. However, he begs and whines to the point where she allows him to play outside without his completing his work.

Circle the correct response:

Negative reinforcement   Positive reinforcement

Which behaviors are being reinforced?

_____

_____

_____

---

to a situation in which a negative event is occurring and the person's behavior will get rid of it, whether it's tension, boredom, a child's whining or throwing a tantrum, or a dog barking.

Before you can intervene with reinforcement, you first have to identity the contingencies occurring in the environment. Once you have, there are several options for intervention.

1. Educate the client on the reinforcement pattern that is occurring.

Example #1: "You probably haven't been aware of it, but every time you smoke marijuana to deal with your boredom, you are actually increasing the likelihood next time that you'll use marijuana the next time you are bored."

EXERCISE 3.2: DEVELOPING ALTERATIVE REINFORCERS

Behavior	Potential Existing Reinforcers	Alternate Reinforcers
Man hitting his partner	Feels a reduction in tension Gets partner to stop questioning where he goes after work Re-establishes power in the relationship after feeling humiliated	The man is taught to reduce his tension through other ways, such as deep breathing, progressive muscle relaxation, and taking timeouts when his frustration begins to build. The man learns alternative communication skills so he can get his needs met by talking rather than hitting.
Cocaine use	May be positively reinforced by the resultant feelings of well-being and enjoyable social interaction with others.	A person with a cocaine problem is given tokens that can be exchanged for rewards, like movie tickets, when she has a clean urinalysis in an intervention called community reinforcement training.
A child who doesn't do schoolwork or chores	May be reinforced if it means attention, even if it is yelling or criticism, from adults.	Teachers and parents are taught to praise and give privileges for finishing work.
Your Example:		

Example #2: "Your child might get something out of arguing about the rules you've set. When you start to justify them and explain them repeatedly, he is enjoying the attention he receives."

2. Help the client stop a problematic reinforcement pattern from occurring, usually with extinction. (Extinction is explained in more detail later in this chapter.)
3. Identify behaviors that the client wants to see, and develop reinforcements around those. Examples follow below and then there is space for you to practice a similar process. See Exercise 3.2.

TYPES OF POSITIVE REINFORCEMENT

Positive reinforcement is the foundation for operant behavior interventions. Types of reinforcement systems commonly used are social reinforcement, high-probability behaviors, and token economies. These all act to increase the frequency of a behavior's occurrence. The social worker should know about these so they can be employed to help people reach desired behaviors.

SOCIAL REINFORCEMENT

Social reinforcement, namely praise and complimenting, is discussed first because it is the easiest type to apply and is already within most people's repertoire. In addition, any other reinforcement system will typically use social reinforcement along with it. Social reinforcement involves praise, smiles, winks, thumbs-up signs, hugs, and pats on the head or shoulder. Some of the guidelines for praise are similar to the general guidelines for reinforcement, but also include the following (Webster-Stratton, 2012):

- Express praise immediately after the behavior is performed instead of waiting too long to do so.
- Praise effort and progress rather than just achievement or perfection.
- Label praise (describing specifically what the person has done to deserve praise so the person knows what behaviors to repeat) instead of making global statements, such as "What a good boy!"
- Couple verbal praise with eye contact, a smile, and/or physical affection.
- Avoid praise followed by criticism ("You did a good job washing the dishes, but why can't you dry them right?").
- Avoid arguing about the praise and ignore inappropriate responses. For instance, if a child protests in reaction to praise ("I did not do a good job, why are you lying to me?"), simply ignore the provocation.

HIGH-PROBABILITY BEHAVIORS

High-probability behaviors are defined as behaviors in which people naturally engage, such as playing outside, using a cell phone, using the Internet, playing video games, and watching TV. High-probability behaviors should be considered because they don't involve setting up a complicated system; instead, one can rely on behaviors that are already present. An example of using high-probability behaviors for reinforcement is a person who allows herself to watch TV only after she exercises. High-probability behaviors can generally be set up as "when/then" conditions, as in "*When* you do your homework, *then* you can play video games."

TOKEN ECONOMIES

Another type of reinforcement system involves *token economies,* in which points or tokens (stickers, starts, checks, coins) are given for desirable behaviors and are then traded in for agreed-upon rewards. You might already be familiar with token economies from your social work setting. If you work in a residential placement or a treatment facility, points or "levels," in which certain privileges, such as weekends home or field trips, are contingent upon certain behaviors to earn these privileges.

Token economies have a number of advantages:

- They can bridge the gap between the desired behavior and the reward.
- They are a tangible reminder to individuals that they are getting closer to earning their reward.

- Points can be attached to different tasks that may comprise a desired goal when the behavior involved is complex. For instance, getting to school on time comprises several behavioral sequences. Therefore, each sequence can be reinforced rather than waiting until the whole behavior is performed.
- Tokens can be quickly and easily administered without interrupting the desired behavior.
- Tokens are less prone to satiation. When agreed-upon rewards lose their reinforcing value, they can simply be exchanged for other rewards.
- Tokens can also be used for punishment; points can be withdrawn for offensive behaviors.

Different versions of token economy charts are presented in Example 3.3 (community reinforcement for substance use disorder) and (adolescent residential treatment). Use of a token economy in a pediatric setting is illustrated in Example 3.5.

In Exercise 3.3, you are asked to think critically about Example 3.5 and the general use of food as rewards.

Although token economies can be very effective, one drawback is that people have to be organized about implementing them consistently. Potential pitfalls with the use of tokens for children can be avoided by training parents how to use token economies effectively:

- Keep the number of target behaviors to few in number (say, three at the most).
- Target behaviors should be the same for all children in a household, when possible.
- Allow the children to place the check marks (stickers, stars, etc.) on the chart themselves. This process is reinforcing in itself, and this way, children can take more ownership over their behavior.
- Keep the token economy chart in a high-traffic area of the home.

EXAMPLE 3.3: COMMUNITY REINFORCEMENT WITH A TOKEN ECONOMY

Behavior	Week 1	Week 2	Week 3	Week 4	Total
Negative drug-screen 3/week					
Attending AA/NA support groups 3×/week					
Attending relapse prevention groups 3×/week					
Talk to sponsor 3×/week					
Total points/chips per week 12 possible points					**Total 48 possible points**

EXAMPLE 3.4: A TOKEN ECONOMY IN ADOLESCENT RESIDENTIAL TREATMENT

Levels Earned by Points	Behaviors Required to Earn Points
Level 1: 0–15 Phone: 15 minutes Computer access: 1 hour	1. Ability to engage with staff and peers positively
Level 2: 16–45 Open privileges Phone: 30 minutes	2. Participate in all required groups
Level 3: 46–75 Visitors	3. Take all medications as prescribed
Level 4: 76–100 Weekend pass	4. Communicate feelings and needs verbally

EXAMPLE 3.5: BEHAVIORAL PLAN IN A PEDIATRIC MEDICAL SETTING

A social work student helped in the formulation of a behavioral plan for 4-year-old Nina, who is with her family from Guatemala in the United States to have a brain tumor removed. Unfortunately, two surgeries were required to remove it, and now she becomes distraught whenever a medical staff member touches her. Before the surgery, Nina was blind in one eye due to the tumor; since the surgeries she has become completely blind. Given her experiences in the hospital, Nina has become increasingly antagonistic toward doing anything. Specifically, at her physical therapy session, she would throw a tantrum at the beginning of the session and refuse to comply. During her physical therapy sessions, her parents, the physical therapists, and the intern were positively reinforcing her by cheering Nina on for even the smallest efforts, but clearly something else was called for.

The social work intern sat down with her supervisors to try to improve the sessions, and decided that food was an appropriate reinforcer, since Nina couldn't see stickers or other visual rewards, and the hospital setting had its own limitations regarding positive reinforement.

(continued)

Behavioral Plan

Tasks	Requirements and Rewards
Walking down the hallway to help her with walking and balance	Nina has to walk from her bed down the short hallway to the physical therapy room. She gets M&Ms along the way, about every 5 feet.
Playing the keyboard to help with spatial relations	The keyboard has five large keys colored yellow, red, blue, green, and purple. The keyboard has different settings: it either plays music or speaks the colors that are struck. The therapist puts the keyboard on the color mode and has Nina hit all of the colors. Then she has Nina find all of the colors by saying, "Find red" or "Find purple." Every time she finds the right color, she gets that color M&M. First she finds all the colors with one hand a few times, then she uses her other hand. Then she plays the music setting with both hands, getting M&M's for each correct color named.
Opening and closing toy balls	Balls are put next to Nina when she sits down. She opens and closes each one to retrieve the M&M inside. She then takes rocks and puts those inside each of the three balls, for which she receives an M&M each.

After a couple of weeks, Nina walked much more easily. She was also more comfortable with her personal space and doing things for herself, such as feeding herself and playing with dolls or stuffed animals. On her own, she decided she wanted to stop wearing diapers and start going to the bathroom instead, as she had before the brain surgery.

EXERCISE 3.3: CRITICAL THINKING QUESTION

What do you see as potential problems in giving children food for reinforcement or rewards?

Explain your reasoning for why you think it was appropriate or inappropriate in the example above.

If you think it was inappropriate, how else could you have designed this behavioral system?

REWARDS

The terms *reinforcement* and *rewards* are often used interchangeably, but they are actually different concepts. Reinforcement, by definition, increases the behavior that precedes it, whereas a reward is something given in return for a service or achievement that may or may not increase the frequency of a behavior (Kazdin, 2012). A common example given to illustrate the difference involves a paycheck versus sales incentives. A paycheck does not necessarily increase "work behavior" (i.e., it doesn't affect the amount of work you do). However, if you are given a monetary incentive for certain quotas of sales, then you may be motivated to work harder in order to get the incentive.

Although these operant behavioral techniques have been presented here in a fairly straightforward manner, understand that when you are training parents, they typically will pose objections to many aspects of positive reinforcement and their accompanying rewards. Some ways to counter parental objections are offered here in Table 3.2. More information on how to work collaboratively with parents and other clients is offered in Chapter 10.

TABLE 3.2: Common Parental Objections to the Use of Reinforcement and Rewards

Common Parental Objections	Social Worker Response
They are too much trouble to create and maintain.	Acknowledge that it would take an initial investment, but the goal would be to progressively shape the behavior, eventually phasing out tokens as the children get closer to the desired outcome.
A reward system is "fake." The "real world" doesn't work like that.	It is true that rewards or tokens are not forthcoming in every setting. However, in many settings, such as the children's school, token economies are being used already. Additionally, we as adults often expect rewards (like a paycheck, for example) for our behavior.
Children will be given too many things without having to earn them.	Explain that rewards and praise actually do need to be earned, but we need to be good at recognizing behaviors that we want to reward.
Praise will lead to lowered expectations.	Praise helps children know what behaviors you want to see more of.
Praise will weaken respect for authority.	Using rewards and praise doesn't mean that you're not still firm. By using praise effectively it can increase respect for authority by demonstrating your ability to be firm and to acknowledge good behaviors.
May require learning new skills when communicating praise.	It may seem difficult at first, but we can practice these skills together until you feel comfortable with it.
Praise may be seen as permission to revert to bad behavior.	While this might happen at first, children will soon learn that in order to receive praise and rewards, they need to consistently demonstrate good behavior.
Rewards get equated with material objects and will be too expensive.	Rewards don't need to be things that we buy. Often the most powerful reinforcers are our praise and attention.

EXTINCTION

Extinction is a fancy word for ignoring. In behavioral terms, extinction involves the process of no longer reinforcing a behavior, resulting in a decrease in the behavior or its possible eradication (Kazdin, 2012). In a previous example, a child's whining was negatively reinforced when it resulted in his getting out of doing homework. Ignoring the whining breaks the connection between the whining and getting out of doing homework.

One guideline for ignoring is that the reinforcer maintaining the behavior must be known, and it has to be under another person's control (Kazdin, 2012). An example illustrating this is a child misbehaving in school. Is the child misbehaving because he gets sent to the principal's office (gets out of class), or is he misbehaving so that he gets the teacher's attention? In the former case, extinction would involve not allowing the child to leave the class no matter how onerous his behavior becomes. In the latter case, extinction involves withdrawing attention from the child when he misbehaves.

Ignoring means literally not talking to the person and not making eye contact. It might even involve leaving the room. For instance, in the example of the child whining to get out of his homework, a parent may have to leave the room so that ignoring can be successful. Of course, this might not be feasible in some situations; a teacher can't leave a classroom to ignore a child.

One important guideline to remember for ignoring is that it works in a gradual way. Although there are some lucky instances when results are immediate, generally people who are being ignored will keep at the behavior for a while because it has worked so well for them in the past. That is the powerful nature of reinforcement at work.

Indeed, when one is teaching ignoring or enacting it, one must understand the concept of an "extinction burst." Expecting to elicit the reinforcement that used to work for the person, he or she might redouble efforts to obtain it. It becomes extremely uncomfortable for the person continuing to ignore a behavior in the face of it escalating (for instance, a child whose whining behavior is being extinguished might now cry, scream, and throw a tantrum). The positive aspect to an extinction burst is that it signals that the extinction process is working. It is the "dark before the dawn." Of course, ignoring should also be accompanied by positive reinforcement for appropriate behaviors (Kazdin, 2012).

Webster-Stratton (2012) also suggests the technique of distraction paired with ignoring for young children. For instance, if Freddy cries because he wants to play with the remote control, rather than shouting at him, his mother could take the remote control away and divert his attention to a brightly colored ball: "Here's something else you can play with. See if you can catch it!"

PUNISHMENT

Punishment involves the presentation or removal of events that decrease the occurrence of a response (Kazdin, 2012). Note the contrast to reinforcement, which involves *increasing* a response through the presentation of an event. Types of punishment include the following:

1. Presentation of undesirable consequences (physical discipline, harsh words, criticism)
2. Removal of desired events, objects, privileges

Guidelines for offering punishment of children are presented in Table 3.3, and those specific to timeout for child behavior problems are given in Table 3.4.

Parents, especially those who are mandated to services, can be defensive about their use of physical punishment. Simply telling people that they should use the discipline methods named here is insufficient. Therefore, a collaborative discussion, centering on parents' beliefs and feelings about physical punishment, their perceptions of risk and benefits, and the effects on the family, is often warranted (see Table 3.5).

Further, the caseworker must be sensitive to cultural beliefs about the appropriateness of physical punishment. The matter has been subject to mixed findings and debate, but African-American families may be more likely to endorse physical punishment as a legitimate means of discipline (Gershoff, 2002; Gershoff, Lansford, Sexton, Davis-Kean, & Sameroff, 2012). Forehand and Kotchick (1996) state that, for various historical reasons, African-American parents socialize their children for obedience to authority and to become "tough" to handle difficult and discriminatory environments, which is often achieved through physical punishment.

TABLE 3.3: Guidelines for Punishment of Children

- Punishment should be applied, if possible, using a calm and controlled demeanor.
- Punishment and consequences should immediately follow the undesired behavior.
- Punishment and consequences should be something that the responsible adult can feasibly and easily implement. If not, the adult may be less likely to follow through on the consequence.
- Punish the behavior every time it occurs until the behavior occurs only at low levels; then it is acceptable to punish intermittently.
- Increased intensity of punishment does not translate into more learning.
- Punishments should be ones that parents can maintain. (For instance, working parents often ground a child as punishment, even though they are not home in the afternoons to enforce this.)
- Verbal punishments, if used frequently, tend to lose their impact over time if they are not accompanied by other consequences.

TABLE 3.4: Guidelines for Timeout

- Create a place that is free from reinforcement, meaning there should be no activities available, and the child is to do nothing.
- Attempts by the child to engage other family members should be ignored.
- If behavior escalates and becomes too disruptive during timeout, delay the punishment until behavior is under control and then resume timeout, extending the time.
- Rules for timeout should be structured, particularly around a time frame. A general guideline is one minute in timeout for each year of the child's age.
- After the timeout is over, the child needs to recount the reason for the timeout and what the child plans to do differently next time.

TABLE 3.5: Collaborative Conversations About the Use of Physical Punishment

Exploratory Questions	Typical Parent Reactions	Sample Practitioner Responses
"Tell me how spanking works for you."	"Spanking is the only thing that makes my children listen."	Join with the goal of authoritative parenting (having clear and consistent rules and monitoring children's whereabouts and activities). "How much do you want your child's compliance to be based on fear? If they fear you, will your children come to you with questions, concerns, and their feelings?"
"How often do you use it?"	"Only when they don't mind any other way, as a last resort."	If parents resort to physical punishment "only when they have to," they train their children to disobey until they are hit (the parent is being negatively reinforced).
"How do you feel afterward?"	Reduction in tension, satisfaction, guilt	While the original purpose of punishment is to reduce noncompliance and teach appropriate behavior, in actuality, negative reinforcement, the satisfaction parents get from "teaching the child a lesson," the reduction of parental frustration, and the exacting of "revenge" to the child all play larger roles.
"Do you ever feel you lose control when you spank?"	Some parents will admit to this.	Reflect the guilt and the desire to refrain from truly hurting their children and being in trouble with authorities.
"Does spanking make your child behave in other settings, such as school or daycare?"	Parents often admit it does not.	Children often won't obey in other places where they are not getting hit, since the effects don't generalize.
"What does your child learn from hitting?"	Parents usually say they learn to behave.	Parents model aggression and children are more likely to hit others and to lie to avoid being hit. It doesn't teach good behavior, only what not to do.
What are the effects of physical punishment?	Some parents will say that it helps build character; some will say fear.	The practitioner can cite some of the research: As well as injury, the short-term consequences of physical abuse include the externalization of problems, such as through anger, aggression, (Turner, Finkelhor, & Ormrod, 2006), and delinquency (Gilbert, Widom, Browne, Webb, & Janson, 2009), and the internalization of problems, such as in depression (Turner, 2006). Long-term consequences include PTSD (Briere & Elliott, 2003). Youth who have been maltreated are also more at risk for violent injuries and death (Lee & White, 2012) and are at increased risk of arrest, general and violent offending, and illicit drug use in young adulthood (Smith, Ireland, & Thornberry, 2005).

(continued)

TABLE 3.5: Continued

Exploratory Questions	Typical Parent Reactions	Sample Practitioner Responses
"If you were physically punished as a child, how did you feel about it?" A follow-up question here is: "How would you like things to be different for your child than how they were for you?"	Responses vary here. Some parents will defend their own parents, saying they made the right choice, whereas others will admit they felt humiliated, scared, and/or angry.	Some people are responsive to reflecting on how they were treated as a child and how they would like their children's lives to be different.

CONCLUSION

This chapter has covered the explanation of operant conditioning and the application of its techniques. The focus has been on populations and problems with which social work is involved, so you can see its relevance to today's practice environment. This chapter has emphasized that operant conditioning can be a powerful tool when the social worker can either control the reinforcement schedule for a client's behavior or teach people to use reinforcement for another people's behavior. In the latter situation, it is important that social workers deliver such information in a collaborative fashion; otherwise, people will not implement the techniques in the way they are constructed. More details on promoting collaboration are offered in Chapter 10.

TEST YOUR SKILLS EXERCISE 3.2: OPERANT CONDITIONING

Exercise Instructions: Circle the correct answers to the questions and statements below.

1. The following are all examples of negative reinforcement EXCEPT:
   a. A child learns that if he throws a tantrum his mother gives in.
   b. A mother learns that if she gives in to her child's tantrums, then he will stop being an embarrassment to her in public.
   c. Avoiding social contact so that one does not have to suffer disappointment and pain.
   d. Avoiding situations that make one anxious.

(continued)

2. Parent training relies heavily on the following EXCEPT:
   a. Positive reinforcement
   b. Modeling
   c. Behavior rehearsal
   d. Respondent conditioning
3. Parent training falls under what type of learning paradigm primarily?
   a. Operant conditioning
   b. Respondent conditioning
   c. Cognitive therapy
   d. Social learning
4. Problems can be addressed through operant conditioning methods EXCEPT:
   a. Child behavior problems
   b. Substance use disorders
   c. Anxiety
   d. Depression (behavior activation)
5. Punishment is different from negative reinforcement in which way?
   a. It follows an aversive behavior.
   b. It results in the decrease of a behavior.
   c. It results in the increase of a behavior.
   d. It is the only way that children learn.
6. In which setting might it be more difficult for a social worker to directly apply operant conditioning techniques with clients?
   a. Long-term nursing facilities
   b. Inpatient hospitals
   c. Schools
   d. Outpatient mental health
7. A child makes distracting noises while a teacher is talking until the teacher reprimands him. While he stops after she has just reprimanded him, he keeps making a nuisance of himself in class. Which of the following is an accurate representation of positive or negative reinforcement for the adult and child?
   a. The child receives negative reinforcement, as a result of the reprimand from the teacher.
   b. The teacher and child each receive positive reinforcement.
   c. The child receives positive reinforcement and the teacher receives negative reinforcement.
   d. The teacher receives positive reinforcement and the child receives negative reinforcement.

(continued)

8. A woman in a violent relationship has left her partner. However, she now misses him and feels very alone. She returns to him, and he is very remorseful and treats her well; they both feel intensely happy. Which behavioral principles best explain her staying in the relationship?

    a. Negative reinforcement (her feelings of loss are terminated by going back with him, which reinforces her staying with him) and positive reinforcement (he positively reinforces her for returning to him).

    b. Positive and negative reinforcement. The woman feels intensely happy, but is in a relationship with the potential to continue to be violent.

    c. Positive reinforcement would only be present if he bought her gifts; negative reinforcement is when she is slapped for being critical of him.

    d. None of these explain why she stays in the relationship.

9. Which of the following aspects of drinking involve negative reinforcement?

    a. Anxiety about talking to people one does not know at a social gathering

    b. Boredom-induced drinking

    c. Feeling bonded to others when drinking and in talking about one's drinking escapades later

    d. Feeling hung over after a drinking binge

    e. Both (a) and (b)

10. Tammy has a close friend who is frequently complaining about not having enough money. It makes Tammy very upset, especially because she has a very tight budget of her own and often will end up giving money to her friend because she feels guilty. Tammy has determined that that she needs to do something different because she still wants to spend time with her friend. She has decided that she will not respond to her friend when she starts talking about the topic of money. This is a good example of which operant conditioning technique?

    a. Nonadherence

    b. High-probability behaviors

    c. Extinction

    d. Behavioral activation

CHAPTER 4

ASSESSMENT, GOAL-SETTING, AND EVALUATION

With learning about classical and operant conditioning, the original parts of behavioral theory, the critical importance of measurement and operationalization becomes apparent, arising from the research tradition of behavioral theory. CBT is very concerned with precise identification of behaviors and goals, as well as with tracking these over time. This chapter covers the assessment and definition of behaviors and goals. It also discusses how to evaluate client progress using these indicators, to determine when intervention has been successful.

ASSESSMENT OF PROBLEMS

One of the initial aspects of a behavioral assessment is to gather concrete manifestations of the problem and its immediate context (see Table 4.1), rather than accepting people's often general descriptions. You can do this by getting people to discuss a specific incident that occurred, usually in terms of an incident that was typical; a recent incident; or one that was particularly severe. Assessment can then proceed to gathering information about the cues (Chapter 2) and reinforcements (Chapter 3) of a behavior in a biopsychosocial behavioral assessment (Chapter 8).

SELF-MONITORING

In order to foster the client's more conscious control over the behavior and to gain insight into the motives behind the behavior, clients can use self-monitoring during the time between your contacts with them. Sometimes self-monitoring alone will result in a reduction of behavior as people become more aware of their behavioral patterns. A number of self-monitoring tools for a range of problems (e.g., substance use, overeating, and anxiety)

TABLE 4.1: Behavioral Assessment of the Problem

When?
What's the typical timing (time of day, week, month, or year) of the problem?
How often do you experience the problem (once an hour, once a day, once a week)?
How long does it last?

Where?
Where are you when it occurs?
What is it about the setting that contributes to the problem?

What?
What are you doing when the problem occurs?
What are you telling yourself?
What bodily reactions are you experiencing?

Who?
Who is there?
What are they doing or saying?

---

are available in Exercise 4.1. The U.K. getselfhelp website also offers free and low-cost cell phone applications for clients who prefer technological delivery.

As well as these resources, many treatment manuals offer self-monitoring as a beginning stage of intervention. For instance, in a manual for treating anger problems and substance use disorder, Reilly and Shopshire (2002) describe the anger meter as a way to monitor one's level of anger. A "1" represents a complete lack of anger or a state of calm, whereas a "10" represents an angry and explosive loss of control that leads to negative consequences. Points between 1 and 10 indicate feelings of anger between these extremes. The purpose of the meter is to monitor the escalation of anger. As people become more aware of their anger building, they can learn strategies to deal with high-risk situations.

EXERCISE 4.1: SELF-MONITORING AS HOMEWORK

- http://www.psychologytools.org/download-therapy-worksheets.htm
  http://www.getselfhelp.co.uk/freedownloads2.htm http://www.getselfhelp.co.uk/freedownloads.htm

  Using one of the above websites, choose a self-monitoring form that may be applicable to one of your clients. Discuss why you chose the particular form and how you will introduce the form to your client and follow up with its use.

  _____

  _____

  _____

The other general purpose of self-monitoring is to better establish a baseline of a behavior. Goals are set with these initial baselines in mind. For instance, if a person discovers that she spends an average of an hour a day picking her skin compulsively, a reasonable goal would be to reduce this behavior by a certain percentage. Establishing a baseline is important so that the goal chosen is realistic and achievable based on current functioning. Discussion of goals is the topic of the next section.

GOAL-SETTING

Goals are defined in a way that allows us to assess whether they are met as the client proceeds through intervention. If a client's behavior does not seem to be responding to the intervention, then we can modify the intervention to make it more helpful to the client. Table 4.2 offers some guidelines on how to speak about the necessity of goals for clients and some ideas to

TABLE 4.2: Guidelines for Goal-Setting

Guideline	Rationale	Examples/Sample Dialogue
Explain the rationale for goals.	To provide focus to the work. To get the social worker and the client to reach agreement on what should be done. To monitor progress of the intervention. To know when the work is complete.	"In order for us to know that this is helpful, we need to make sure we are in agreement on what I am helping you work toward. To do that, we need to set some goals, things that you want to get out of this treatment and the way you want your life to look as a result of coming here. That way, we will also know when you have received what you came here for."
Explain how intervention targets the individual.	When a client wants another person to change, explain that your parameter of influence expands only to the client. Clients can learn new behaviors that will influence other people to act differently. However, if it is appropriate, you may involve others in the intervention (for instance, a partner or a parent).	"Unfortunately, I can only work with you on what you can do differently in the relationship. I am not able to influence another person unless he or she is in the room as well."
Goals should be considered in terms of final outcome rather than the formal services in which clients participate.	To develop a mindset toward outcome rather than simply "going through the motions" of attending different services.	Rather than attending a parenting skills group, the goal should focus on what the parent is expected to achieve as a result of attending the group. Attendance at the group is then the means by which the parent may achieve the goal.

(continued)

Guideline	Rationale	Examples/Sample Dialogue
Formulate a minimum number of goals.	Prioritize goals around the client's input.	"Which of these goals is most important for you to center on? Which one would make the most difference to you right now?"
Goals should be feasible considering their baseline behaviors.	To set up a person for success, the progress needed to achieve the goal cannot be too far from the current baseline.	If a child's conduct in school is rated as unsatisfactory every day of the week, then a goal of five satisfactory days would be out of his reach. Perhaps an achievable beginning goal might be two satisfactory days.
State goals as the presence of positive behaviors rather than the absence of negative behaviors whenever possible.	The social worker must continue to be persistent, since clients will often continue to talk about the absence of negatives (e.g., "I don't know—he just won't be talking back.").	Rather than being stated as "stopping talking back at school," the goal should be phrased as "complying with directions," by asking, "What will you be doing instead of [the problem behavior]?"
If it is necessary to focus on reducing a behavior, such as the frequency or duration of temper tantrums, then also create replacement goals.	In this way, the client is not focusing on what he or she is not supposed to do, but on what he or she can do instead, which is more motivating and achievable.	Some replacement goals to put into place instead of throwing a tantrum include talking about frustrations and other feelings rather than acting them out.
Determine the client's level of commitment to the goal.	Commitment or motivation to a certain goal can be determined quickly through the use of a scale.	"On a scale from 1 to 10, with 1 being not at all important and 10 being very important, where would you place yourself?"

Sources: Christensen, Todahl, & Barrett, 1999; Hepworth et al., 2012

help with their formulation. Exercise 4.2 asks you to apply the guidelines provided to brief scenarios and to describe how you would help clients develop the goals they present.

Once goals have been introduced and discussed, they can be phrased in a precise way so that both workers and clients are clear about where efforts should lie and they will "know when they get there." The client is clear about what he or she is working toward and knows when the goal has been reached. One way to cultivate behavioral specificity is to ask, "Pretend I am taping you on video. What will you be doing that I can see when I look through the camera?" Table 4.3 presents other questions that may stimulate a client to consider goals for your work together.

A final goal formulation will include a definition of the behavior to be changed and the level of desired change. The level of desired change can be considered in terms of frequency, duration, or intensity (Cormier, Nurious, & Osborn, 2009); these are detailed in Exercise 4.3.

EXERCISE 4.2: LEARNING TO DEVELOP CLIENT GOALS

Exercise Instructions: Read the scenarios listed below and respond on the right.

Goal Scenario:	How would you develop the goal?
A client who is suffering from depression says that she just wants to feel happier.	
A mother names her goal as "My family needs to communicate better."	
An adolescent girl seen by a social work intern placed at a juvenile justice detention center says she doesn't have any goals for herself and doesn't want to work on anything.	
A man whose girlfriend broke up with him because of his physical violence says that his goal is "for her to take me back."	
A parent whose 7-year-old child has been acting out at home and at school (shooting spitballs, laughing and making loud jokes to the classroom at large, talking when the teacher is talking, not doing work) says that her goal is for the social worker to "talk some sense into him" and "make him see right."	
A man who has been referred for substance use disorder treatment says his goal is to quit drinking.	
A woman says that her goal is to "be married."	
A man says his goal is "to get a job."	
A seventh-grader who is being seen by the school social work intern is currently not doing any homework (he usually gets four homework assignments per day). The school social work intern decides that his goal should be "to do all his homework."	
A child protective services worker writes up her initial quarterly case plan. She decides that the client's goals should be to (1) seek better housing; (2) attend a battered women's group; (3) participate in a parenting skills group; and (4) receive job skills training. For the client's child, who has been diagnosed with autism, the caseworker draws up some other goals that involve the mother: (1) to seek services at a clinic that specializes in pervasive developmental disorders, and (2) to attend a support group related to her child's disability.	

How would you like things to be better?

What specifically are you hoping to change?

What will it look like when you've made the change you want? What will you be doing, saying, and thinking?

How will people be reacting to you? What will you be saying to each other and doing with each other?

EXERCISE 4.3: DEFINING MEASUREMENT OF CLIENT BEHAVIORS

Exercise Instructions: The level of change is defined and examples are provided here. Please include a relevant example from your own practice.

Level of Change	Definition	Measure	Example	Your Example
Frequency	Number of times	Count	Number of positive thoughts, number of social outings	
Duration	Period of time over which a behavior that is not discrete and lasts for varying amounts of time occurs.	Time	If a child is currently doing no homework, he may increase it by 30 minutes. If a person is experiencing cravings for 2 hours a day, this is reduced to 1 hour a day.	
Intensity	Degree to which an emotion is experienced (pervasiveness, strengths, amount it interferes with other experiences)	Ratings such as Subjective Units of Disturbance or Distress, first created by Wolpe (1969). It is usually constructed as a 1–10 scale, with 1 meaning "no distress" and 10, "severe distress."	Reducing the intensity of depression on a daily basis, from an 8 to a 5.	

TASK-SETTING

After goals have been identified, tasks—specific steps in service of goals—can be formulated. In other words, "What do you need to do in order to achieve the goal you've set for yourself?" Cormier et al. (2009) suggest brainstorming with the client to come up with a list of tasks, ranking easiest to hardest. Example 4.1 details such a list for a woman whose goal was to find a job, and Exercise 4.4 gives you practice in establishing tasks to meet a goal.

EXAMPLE 4.1: LIST OF CLIENT SUBGOALS AND TASKS

Client whose goal is to find a job:
1. Search city job website for jobs.
2. Search county job website for jobs.
3. Call my friend at the agency to see if they're hiring there.
4. Go to company #1's website to see if they have employment postings.
5. Go to company #2's website to see if they have employment postings.
6. Go to company #3's website to see if they have employment postings.
7. Search the classifieds in Sunday's paper.
8. Update my résumé.
9. E-mail my friend to ask her if I can use her as a reference.
10. Call for more information on that company I thought of today.
11. Get the address of the company I worked for 2 years ago.
12. Fill out application #1.
13. Send application #1.
14. Fill out application #2.
15. Send application #2.
16. Fill out application #3.
17. Send application #3

List for a child who has tantrums:
1. Identify signs in his body that he is starting to become frustrated (tension in his muscles, voice getting louder, a hot feeling in his head).
2. Identify signs in his thoughts that he is starting to become frustrated (e.g., "I can't do this!" "I don't want to do this!" "It's too hard.").
3. Verbalize feelings to his parents: "I'm frustrated. I don't know how to do this."
4. Take 5- to 10-minute timeouts to cool off, doing activities that will help him relax (going to his room and making paper airplanes, playing with his Legos and toys, drinking a glass of water, throwing a ball outside).

(continued)

A patient in a long-term care unit who is dependent on a ventilator for his breathing has a goal of getting out of bed two times per week:

1. He will initiate a conversation with the nursing staff regarding when he would like activity to take place.
2. As part of getting out of bed, he will comply with staff requests to move his arm or leg within 5 to 7 seconds.
3. He will remain out of bed and up in his wheelchair for a minimum of 3 hours before requesting to get back in bed.

EXERCISE 4.4: DEVELOPING TASKS

Exercise Instructions: From either a hypothetical example of a goal you provided, or, even better, working directly with a client, develop all the subgoals or tasks that will have to be achieved in order to meet the goal you have come up with.

Goal:

Subgoals or Tasks:

1.
2.
3.
4.
5.

EVALUATION

Evaluation is ongoing from assessment forward. Many times we rely on a client's verbal self-report during our contacts to find out how they are progressing with their goals. However, in CBT other evaluation tools can be used, since they can provide further "objective" evidence about the level of a behavior—and its change—over time. Standardized self-rating scales and self-anchored scales are discussed here.

TABLE 4.4: Resources for Finding Standardized Measures
A Google search
A search in library databases, such as Psychinfo
Corcoran and Fischer (2013) have compiled two volumes of measures for social work.
Mash and Barkley (2009)'s work concentrates on child and adolescent problems.
Early and Newsome (2005) discuss measures that emphasize strengths.

STANDARDIZED SCALES

A measure helps determine the existence of certain behaviors, attitudes, feelings, or qualities—and their magnitude—in clients when they come to a social work practitioner for assistance. An inventory (the words *measure, inventory, instrument,* and *scale* are used interchangeably) is standardized when it has been tested (normed) on a relevant group of people, a process that results in psychometric data—specifically, information about reliability and validity—that have to meet certain acceptable standards. *Reliability* refers to the consistency and the accuracy of the measure, and *validity* involves the extent to which the instrument measures what it purports to measure.

Standardized measures can be completed by the client (self-report); by an important collateral person who can make key observations about the client's behavior, attribute, or attitude (a parent, teacher, or spouse, for example); or by the practitioner using an observational measure. Table 4.4 provides a list of resources for finding standardized measures.

SELF-ANCHORED SCALES

Self-anchored scales are also a useful way for clients to assess their current level of a behavior and how it changes in response to intervention. First created by Wolpe (1969), the Subjective Units of Disturbance or Distress scale (SUD), asks the client to rate the intensity of a feeling, such as anxiety. They are constructed as either a 1-to-100 or a 1-to-10 scale, with 1 connoting "no distress" and 10 "severe distress." The SUD rating is used to establish a baseline and as a quick measure to administer over time to see how intervention influences the problem.

Scaling questions, although taken from solution-focused therapy (deJong & Berg, 2012), encapsulate a number of processes that cognitive behaviorists find important, in addition to the measurement of baseline, progress, and outcome. They also have the benefit of reducing problems that people perceive as overwhelming into manageable proportions, concentrating on only one problem at a time.

The following process entails scale questions (deJong & Berg, 2012) which I have adapted into language that is more compatible with a cognitive-behavioral approach. The scale used in the example presented here is for Luis, 14-year-old Latino male who is on probation for assault.

- Choosing a goal for the scale
- Anchoring the goal with behaviors and thoughts
- Generating alternative perspectives

- Formulating between-session tasks
- Measurement

CONSTRUCT A SCALE AROUND A GOAL

Verbally and in writing, describe a 1-to-10 scale around a goal you have developed with the client. Phrase the goal in terms of the presence of a positive behavior but not one that is expressed in superlative terms. For example, if a person is depressed, talking about "feeling full of joy" might be seen as too extreme and unrealistic.

Example: Luis originally talked about "not being bad anymore" as his initial goal. When the intern prompted, "What will you be doing instead?" he was able to elaborate that he would be "living in peace."

ANCHOR THE GOAL

Anchor 10 as the outcome—when the goal will be achieved, when "the problem is no longer a problem," or "when the problem you came for here is solved." A focus on 10 allows clients, who previously may have viewed their problems as "hopeless" and "overwhelming," to concretely see the possibility of change, which gives them hope for the future. To operationalize the goal, ask clients to describe in concrete and specific terms at least three behaviors and thoughts they will be having when they have reached 10.

Intern: Luis said he would be "walking away" from escalating arguments and avoiding "people who got on his nerves." He would be thinking, "I'm not going to let someone looking for a fight ruin my record."

RANK ORDERING AND EXCEPTION-FINDING

Clients then rank themselves in relation to 10. Clients will often place themselves at a number that implies change has already occurred, and this can be used to help them see that their problems are not as all-encompassing as they had previously believed and that the client has drawn on some resources. You can inquire about these strengths and compliment them.

Occasionally, clients will place themselves at a 1. In these cases, the practitioner can ask what the client is doing to prevent problems from getting even worse. You will be surprised to find that people are always taking advantage of some resources. It is important that you not challenge people on their ratings. For instance, you would not say, "A 7? You are not!" The way to get at any discrepancy is to ask about the perspective of other people, which is covered in the next section.

Example: When Luis was asked where he would place himself on the scale now, he said "probably at a 4." He said that since he'd been on probation, he'd employed the strategies he'd already named—walking away from potential trouble, avoiding such situations, and telling himself that basically he was in control of his record, not other people.

GENERATE ALTERNATIVE PERSPECTIVES

This involves asking people to rate themselves on their scale from the viewpoint of another person who is invested in their change. Very often clients will view themselves differently from how others experience them. Getting clients to perceive themselves from someone else's perspective may help them see themselves more realistically.

Example: Luis said that his probation officer would rank him at a 3, because he didn't know the inner resolve it had taken to make Luis decide that he was not going to get in further trouble and to follow through with some actions.

SET TASKS

Here clients are asked to determine how they will move up one rank order by the time of the next contact: "So what will you do between now and the next time I see you to move one number up on the scale?"

Example: Luis said that he could attend the adolescent support group his probation officer had referred him to. When asked what he was supposed to get out of his attendance, he admitted, "I don't really know. He just said I should go, that it would look good to the judge." He agreed that he would ask his probation officer the purpose of the group. "Maybe then I won't have to go if I show him I'm already doing that stuff." He also came up with the idea of making a phone call to the agency that sponsored the support group to sign up for it.

MEASURE PROGRESS

The scale should be preserved in the case file and a copy given to the client. At each contact, the practitioner can check in regarding where clients rank themselves on their scale and on their completion of tasks. Progress continues to be monitored, which makes attainment toward goals quantifiable and measurable.

TEST YOUR SKILLS EXERCISE 4.1: EVALUATING TOOLS

Exercise Instructions: Choose one of the tools for evaluation presented in this chapter and answer the questions below.

Which tool did you select?

What made you choose it?

How did you present it to the client?

Were there any difficulties in presentation? If there were, what would you have done differently?

What did you find out from using the scale?

What did you share with the client about your results?

How will you use it to evaluate progress with the client?

SECTION THREE

COGNITIVE MODELS

CHAPTER 5

COGNITIVE RESTRUCTURING

Behavioral theory is focused on overt behaviors that can be observed and measured. By the early 1960s, however, the importance of a person's covert operations, or cognition, was identified as significant to clinical intervention and added to the theory. This broader focus became known as cognitive-behavioral theory. From the perspective of cognitive theory it is conscious thoughts that are the primary determinants of feelings and behavior (Beck, 2011). Thoughts are referred to by many names (Azar, Barnes, & Twentyman, 1988; Dobson & Dozois, 2001):

- Cognitions
- Self-statements
- Beliefs
- Attitudes
- Appraisals
- Assumptions
- Expectations
- Attributions
- Ideas
- Perceptions
- Expectations
- Schemata
- Scripts

According to cognitive theory, many mental, emotional, and behavioral problems are the result of cognitive misperceptions—conclusions that are based too much on habits of thought rather than external evidence—that people have about themselves, other people, and their life situations.

These misconceptions may develop for a couple of reasons. The first is the simplest—the person has not acquired the information necessary to manage a novel situation. This is often evident in the lives of children and adolescents. They face many situations at school, at play, and with their families that they have not experienced before, and they are understandably not sure how to respond. This is also evident when people face life stressors, such as managing children with temperamental problems, caregiving for an older parent, or being a victim of a crime. These people have not acquired information about these events because they have not experienced them. That is why one of the elements of cognitive-behavioral intervention is often psychoeducation about a particular problem (such as traumatic brain injury, bipolar disorder, Alzheimer's disease). The assumption is that information provided to an individual is reassuring and enables them to know what to expect and what they can do about a certain circumstance.

The other source of misperception is rooted in personal schemas, or systematic patterns of thinking, acting, and solving problems. "Schemas contain understandings or assumptions about oneself, others, and the world...that are stored in memory and are activated to help us interpret new experiences" (Cormier et al., 2009, pp. 391–392). Young, Klosko, & Weishaar (2003) discusses certain types of schemas that may result in people experiencing distress and an inability to cope with life events. See Table 5.1 for common problems and the biased thinking patterns that often accompany them.

Conversely, "rational" thinking can be understood as having the following qualities:

1) It is based on external evidence.
2) It is life preserving.
3) It keeps one helpfully directed toward personal goals.

Cognitive interventions focus on present rather than past behavior (Leahy, 1996). The past is important for discovering the origins of a client's thinking patterns, usually learned in childhood from either societal or family transmission, or both. For example, people with eating disorders may talk about societal norms about being thin. However, CBT is encouraging about the nature of change. Since certain beliefs were learned, they can also be unlearned with new, more functional patterns.

COGNITIVE RESTRUCTURING

Cognitive restructuring was formulated from two different schools of cognitive therapy: rational-emotive therapy, by Ellis (Ellis & McLaren, 1998), and cognitive therapy, by Beck

---

TABLE 5.1: Biased Thinking Patterns Associated with Particular Problems

Problem	Biased Thought Pattern
Depression	**Self:** "I'm worthless."
	Others: "People aren't to be trusted."
	Future: "It's hopeless."
Anxiety	**Self:** "I can't handle situations." "I'm going to fail."
	Others: "People are judging me that I'm inferior."
	Future: "If I don't worry, I won't be prepared for what might happen."
Anger	**Self:** "I shouldn't have to put up with inconvenience or frustration."
	Others: "People are out to get me and take advantage of me."
	World: "The world is dangerous and I need to protect myself."

TABLE 5.2: Common Irrational Beliefs

Irrational Beliefs	Examples
Absolute thinking: viewing events in all or nothing way	"Since I know I can't win if I pl€ my friend, I might as well not
Catastrophizing: seeing minor situations as disastrous	A date doesn't call back: "I'm never going to get married."
Low frustration tolerance" inability to put up with minor inconveniences or uncomfortable feelings	Waiting for a stoplight: "This is driving me crazy. I'm never going to get where I'm going."
Overgeneralization: drawing the conclusion that all instances of some kind of situation or event will turn out a particular way because one or two did.	"I went to that one support group in L.A. when I lived there and that didn't help. Therefore, I won't go to any other groups because they won't help either."
Personal worthlessness: a specific form of overgeneralization associated with failure	An individual is worthless if the house isn't spotless.

Source: A. T. Beck, Cognitive Therapy and the Emotional Disorders. New York: Guilford, 1976

(Beck, 1976; Beck & Freeman, 1990). Both schools share the assumption that problematic reactions result from interpretations of situations that are often negative or illogical (as described in Table 5.1). Certain habitual, patterned ways of thinking over time might lead to the development of particular problems (see Table 5.2 for example). In cognitive restructuring, the social worker assesses the client's patterns of thinking, determines with the client that some of them are not effective for managing important life challenges, and, through a series of discussions and exercises, helps the client to experiment with alternative ways of approaching challenges that will promote goal attainment (Emery, 1985).

STEPS OF COGNITIVE RESTRUCTURING

In clinical assessment, the social worker assesses the client's schema, identifies faulty thinking patterns or cognitive deficits, and considers the evidence supporting the client's conclusions about his or her life situations. When those conclusions seem valid, the social worker initiates a process of problem-solving or teaching of coping skills (see Chapter 7). When the conclusions are distorted, the social worker uses techniques to help clients adjust their cognitive processes in ways that will better facilitate goal attainment. The social worker guides the client through the process, but the client is responsible for implementing these strategies. As thinking changes, so do emotions and behaviors.

In order to change a client's belief systems, the practitioner conducts a four-step process of cognitive-restructuring:

1) Provide information on the connection between thoughts, feelings, and behaviors.
2) Identify the thoughts.
3) Examine the validity of the beliefs.
4) Replace the irrational or problematic thoughts with more functional beliefs.

The first step in cognitive restructuring is to educate the client on the connection between thoughts and feelings, with statements such as the following: "Let's take a look at what you've been saying to yourself. Are you aware that your mind is constantly generating messages? There's a running commentary in the background of our minds. These thoughts we're having influence how we feel and act, even though we might not be very aware of them at first. But we actually have more control over these than you might think, and that is one way we can directly influence the way we feel and act."

Visual diagrams on the connections between feelings, thoughts, and actions may be useful (see Figure 5.1), along with providing an example to illustrate the concepts. A benign example to which most people can relate is getting a flat tire on the way to work. A negative spiral of unhelpful thoughts giving rise to like-minded emotions and behavior may happen if a person reacts to the flat tire by saying to oneself, "Nothing ever works out for me. The whole day is ruined. I'll be late for work now, and I'll probably get fired. I don't know what I'm going to do. I can't stand this." A client will be able to connect that having such thoughts would result in feeling helplessness, hopelessness, frustration, and anxiety. An example such as this one demonstrates that even if thoughts don't directly give rise to feelings, they can influence how we react to a situation.

As a contrast, you can present the option of a client responding to a flat tire in an alternative way: "Well, this is inconvenient, but it happens to everyone at some point. At least I am all right and safe. It's lucky I'm only five blocks away from a garage. I can walk there and get help. I can also call work to tell them what happened. I'll be late. I don't like that this happened, but I'll be able to take care of it."

People are able to see that this response will more likely lead to problem-solving attempts and coping rather than hopelessness, dejection, and stress. The CBT position is that thoughts give direct rise to feelings and reactions.

Clients are educated that cognitive-behavioral therapy works on each of these domains:

ACTIONS are changed by building skills in the areas of social skills, problem-solving, communication, and assertiveness.

FEELINGS are changed by taking different actions (changing behavior), learning relaxation and other coping skills, and changing thoughts.

THOUGHTS are changed by stopping irrational thoughts and increasing positive and productive thoughts. Cognitive restructuring specifically focuses on changing thoughts so that they are more optimistic, or at least realistic. In turn, these optimistic thoughts influence how people feel and behave.

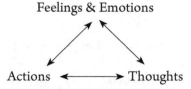

FIGURE 5.1: Visual Connection Between Thoughts, Feelings, and Behaviors

After educating the client on the interconnection of thoughts, feelings, and behaviors, the second step of cognitive restructuring involves helping the person identify the thoughts preceding and accompanying the distressing emotions and nonproductive action (see Table 5.3). Exercise 5.1 provides practice in recognizing distorted thoughts.

As discussed in Chapter 2, often clients confuse thoughts and feelings and, indeed, in speech, people often use the terms interchangeably, Cognitive restructuring requires one to differentiate between the two. A few examples follow on helping clients elicit their cognitions (see Example 5.1). Other ways to get at people's core beliefs that dictate their assumptions and coping responses involve the following questions (Beck, 2005):

What does that mean about you?
What does that mean about others or the world?

After a belief is identified, you can also ask the client about the degree their of belief in that thought:

"What is the degree to which you believe it, from 1 to 10?" As reinforced in Chapter 4, quantification is seen as an aid to assessment, goal-setting, and evaluation of progress.

TABLE 5.3: **Ways to Elicit Clients' Thoughts and Beliefs**

Ways to Get at Cognitions	Sample Statements or Questions
When clients state what they're thinking, the social worker can label or prompt the cognitive process.	"Did you hear what you were telling yourself?"
Ask clients about their cognitive process (Beck, 2005).	"What was going through your mind?" "What were you thinking?" "What were you imagining?" "What were you predicting?" "What were you remembering?" "What did the situation mean to you?" "What was the worst part of the situation?"
Ask about a possibility based on what you already know of the client.	"I wonder if you were thinking, 'She should already know what needs to be done around here. Why do I have to remind her?'"
Provide possibilities, using the thoughts others might have in the situation.	"I've heard from other mothers in this kind of situation that they sometimes think, 'If my caseworker doesn't believe my kids are the most important thing to me, then that means I can't work with her.' Does that sound like what you were thinking?"
Clients who need more tangible ways to grasp their thinking might be asked to do imagery work or role-playing to retrieve the thoughts (Cournoyer, 2010)	"Close your eyes, take a deep breath, and see yourself in that situation. What are you doing? What are you feeling? What are you thinking?"

EXERCISE 5.1: RECOGNIZING DISTORTED THOUGHTS

Exercise Instructions: In the following scenario, indicate where you see some signs of distorted thinking. How can you help the client become aware of these?

Nikki, an 18 year-old white female, came to the university counseling center at the behest of her dormitory floor's residential adviser, who was concerned about Nikki's weight loss. Nikki admitted that she was "not happy" about coming to the center, but she liked the residential adviser and didn't want to "alienate" her. When she came to her initial session, Nikki appeared visibly emaciated and was wearing a long, oversized sweater and baggy sweatpants. At the beginning of the interview, she was guarded and answered questions with only a few words. But when she realized that the social worker "was not going to tell me I needed to gain weight like everyone else," she began to open up, although she spoke in a flat, matter-of-fact tone, even about painful subjects.

Nikki said she had begun to lose weight the summer of her senior year of high school, though her concerns about her weight had begun at age 13. Before that time she had been a "skinny kid," and that's how she wanted to stay. She admitted that she didn't want to grow up and thought that staying thin was a way to achieve this. She said she admired little girls' bodies (even girls as young as 3 and 4), and thought they looked great.

During that summer, Nikki said that she was bored because there were no jobs for high school students in the mid-sized city where she lived. Losing weight gave her "something to do." Every day, she ate only two meals and jumped rope for 30 minutes. If she didn't exercise daily, she felt "fat" and "disgusted" with herself. Nikki said that before the summer, she hadn't had the discipline to cut back on her food intake. At the same time, she said she had exercised and weighed herself almost every day since she was 14 years old. At 5 feet, 4 inches, she has never weighed more than 105 pounds.

Nikki admitted with embarrassment that she did lose control of her eating on occasion, usually with sweet food (ice cream, brownies, cake) but more recently with peanut butter; she could eat an entire jar at one sitting. She said that this happened "maybe once a month" and that she would atone for it by eating even less afterward. She denied using any methods of purging.

When asked how she was feeling during the summer after she finished high school, other than "bored" at the prospect of leaving for college, she seemed surprised by the question and answered, "How did I feel? I didn't feel anything."

(continued)

Since entering college three and a half months ago, Nikki had eaten only two meals a day, subsisting on salad, yogurt, popcorn, and Diet Coke, and had lost an additional 10 pounds (she now weighed 85 pounds). She said that she didn't feel hungry and that the weight loss had been easy. She had also stopped exercising.

Nikki admitted she hadn't menstruated in 7 months and was losing her hair. She didn't mind the lack of menstruation because she had always hated her period, a clear marker that she was a woman. Her hair loss bothered her, however, and she showered only every other day because too much hair fell out when she washed it. She said that occasionally she felt her heart rate "slow down and then speed up." On the one hand, this scared her; on the other hand, she would sometimes think, "Maybe I'll just die of a heart attack, and all this will be over." Despite these physical concerns, she had not been to a doctor.

Nikki said that in one sense she knew she was too thin and wore baggy clothes to disguise the fact, but she still felt "fat inside," recognizing that no amount of weight loss would help her feel different. Yet she didn't know anymore what normal eating was and became panicky when people pressured her about gaining weight. She denied having anorexia to anyone who pushed her about it, saying that she had read the criteria and she hadn't lost 15% of her body weight; therefore, she couldn't have it. If she ever got fat, she said, she would be totally worthless.

Your answer:

EXAMPLE 5.1: IDENTIFYING PROBLEMATIC THOUGHTS AND BELIEFS

Case Example #1: This example involves Ms. Jackson, who is worried about a flare-up of her daughter's sickle cell anemia and suffers from her own anxiety as a result.

Social Work Intern: Now I want you to close your eyes. (Pause.) Picture yourself in your kitchen, where your calendar is. You look up and see that a week has

(continued)

gone by since Toya [youngest daughter] has been in the hospital. Now tell me everything that you're thinking.

Ms. Jackson: I'm getting tight just thinking about it. (Puts her hand on her chest.). I guess I'm thinking, "Here we go again. She's going get sick again and I'm not going be able to handle it. She's going to go to the hospital and never come home. (Speech quickens.) I'm thinking that I should be sick instead of her. She's going to get sick and know that their momma did this to her, that their momma made her feel this pain and hate me because of it."

Case Example #2: In this example, the social work student gets Malcolm, a 36-year-old African American man diagnosed with paranoid schizophrenia, to identify a distorted belief that lies behind his tendency to think he gets financially victimized by others: The student asks him to recall a specific incident that resulted in Malcolm sending the telephone company a check for $300.

Social Work Intern: What were you thinking when you said yes to the sales person's request for the money?

Client: I knew I didn't understand the plan she was talking about, but I didn't want to ask. I didn't think she would tell me the truth anyway.

Social Work Intern: What were you thinking would happen if you did ask her?

Client: She would probably think I was stupid.

Social Work Intern: So, you're on the phone with her and you say yes to her request because you're afraid to ask what she's talking about?

Client: Yeah.

Social Work Intern: And you're afraid to ask because she might think you are stupid?

Case Example #3: In this example, the social worker is helping a white 68-year-old woman who lives in a subsidized housing complex to more consistently receive her Meals on Wheels.

Social Worker: How are you today?

Client: I'm awful. I have all these things I need to do all the time, and no one is helping me.

Social Work Intern: That must feel really lonely and make it so difficult, thinking that no one is helping you with the things you need to do. I'd like us to discuss this thought some more, if that's all right with you.

Client: I guess. I don't know what there is to talk about.

Social Work Intern: Okay. When you say that there is nothing you can do about the fact that some days you can't answer the door for your meals, how does that make you feel?

(continued)

Client: It makes me feel bad.

Social Work Intern: What kind of bad? Can you describe it more specifically?

Client: I feel hopeless. I feel useless. Here they are, bringing me food, and I can't even get out of bed to get it. And then they get mad at me.

Social Work Intern: Let's not worry about them right now, let's stay focused on you. When you're in bed and you hear the knock at the door and you feel hopeless and useless, what are you thinking?

Client: What do you mean?

Social Work Intern: I mean, can you think about the last time this happened, and try to remember the thoughts you had running through your head?

Client: I kept thinking, "It's hopeless" and "I'm useless."

Social Work Intern: What else? Were there any other thoughts in your head?

Client: [Pauses, thinking.] I kept thinking that I want to get out of bed, but I can't. I just don't have the energy. So I'm useless.

Social Work Intern: That must be very painful to think of yourself as useless.

Client: It is, but it's the truth.

EXAMINING THE VALIDITY OF THE BELIEFS

After the beliefs have been identified, they are examined for their validity. The different methods of helping clients appraise whether their thought patterns are realistic are summarized in Table 5.4.

TABLE 5.4: Techniques to Examine the Validity of Beliefs

Examining the evidence	Ask the client to provide evidence for and against the distorted belief.
Considering an alternative perspective	Have the client consider looking at a belief in a different way.
Looking at the worst-case scenario	The client confronts the cognitive distortion of catastrophizing, realizing that the feared negative consequences about a situation are often not as dire as assumed.
Point-counterpoint	The costs and benefits to the client maintaining certain attitudes are covered. Clients begin to get a sense that beliefs and cognitions are not fixed, and thinking becomes more flexible.
Didactic teaching	Didactic teaching means filling in information gaps for clients (Bandura, 1977). The assumption is that cognitions (information) affect the way people feel and behave.
Experiments	Help clients set up natural experiments so they can test the extent to which their beliefs about an event are rational.

EXAMINING THE EVIDENCE

Examining the evidence involves asking the client to provide evidence for and against the distorted belief and is the most common way of uncovering the validity of thoughts (McKay, Davis, & Fanning, 2011). The social worker may pose a series of questions for the client to consider (Creed, Reisweber, & Beck, 2011, p. 74):

- "What tells you that this thought is true? What tells you that it might not be true?"
- "What would your friends say about your thoughts?"

Sometimes clients' irrational thinking revolves around a prediction that a dire event will occur ("If I talk to my boss about my hours, I'll get fired."). In these types of cases, the following questions can be asked:

- When did the feared outcome not happen in the past? What was different about those times?
- What are the odds of the feared outcome occurring? (e.g., crying if one confronts another person about a hurtful behavior)
- How many times in the past has the catastrophe actually happened?

As you can see, the social worker poses a series of deductive questions that cause clients to determine the validity of a belief that may be causing distress. The social worker leads the process (examples of which are provided in Example 5.2.), but the client comes to his or her own conclusions.

EXAMPLE 5.2: EXAMINING THE EVIDENCE

Case Example #1: Maya is a white immigrant from Russia who is the mother of a 10-year-old that has disclosed sexual abuse by her stepfather. Maya fears that she will lose her job.

> **Caseworker:** You've mentioned earlier that you frequently worry about losing your job, right?
>
> **Maya:** Yeah. I mean, things are fine now with money and everything, but I don't know what will happen if I lose my job; I can't imagine what I would do.
>
> **Caseworker:** What do you think the chances are, out of 100%, that you'll lose your job?
>
> **Maya:** I don't know, maybe 40%.

(continued)

Caseworker: Is there a reason that you might be fired or laid off?

Maya: No, but I have been missing work lately.

Caseworker: I can imagine that it must be scary to suddenly be the only bread-winner for your family. Is your supervisor aware of the recent situation with your family?

Maya: Yes, they know. They've been very supportive.

Caseworker: Okay, has your supervisor mentioned to you that he's concerned about the work you've missed?

Maya: No, I have sick days to use.

Caseworker: Has your performance at work deteriorated in any way recently, which would cause your job to be on the line?

Maya: Not really. I know I probably don't deserve to lose my job, but you just never know.

Caseworker: Well, how many people do you know have lost a job for no apparent reason?

Maya: None, I guess.

Caseworker: So what do you think the chances are of you losing your job for any reason within the next year?

Maya: Probably close to 0. (Takes a deep breath.) I guess that's probably not going to happen.

Case Example #2: George, a white man in his early 20s, attends an addiction recovery group held at the halfway house where he is living while he is on probation. Summarizing a recent meeting with his probation officer, he ends by saying, "It's like they're out to get me, looking for a reason to throw me in jail, and with my bad luck, I'm sure they'll find something to get me on." (Note that discussion around negative belief systems by fellow group members who are struggling with similar problems can be productive.)

Leader: What do others hear George expressing?

Al: You're sounding like the victim, but you made the choices that landed you on probation, not bad luck.

Leader: Does anyone else hear that?

Pete: It sounds like you're saying it's out of your hands. Like there's nothing you can do to avoid going to jail, but if you follow the requirements, you won't have to, right?

George: But they think this is the way to do it—to keep me on track by threatening me?

(continued)

Leader: Your probation officer can do anything he wants, but you're the one who makes the choice of how to respond. You can respond negatively and deal with the consequences or you can react positively in a way that will keep you out of jail.

George: But it always seems that something ends up happening and I get in trouble.

Leader: Does something just happen or do you make choices? What does everyone else think?

Jack: I used to think things just happened to me, too—bad luck—and that everyone was against me. But if you try something different, you might not have so much bad luck.

George: But it's always been this way, I never get any breaks. I can't just make them happen.

Leader: What does everyone hear in the language George uses?

Alex: Always, never, can't.

Pete: Self-defeating. It's like you don't even give yourself a chance. You're already telling yourself this is the way it has to be. You're talking yourself into a situation you don't have to choose.

(George nods.)

Leader: You're nodding. Does that mean you can identify with what was just said?

George: I guess I'm just scared.

Leader: I'm sure there are others who are scared in this room.

Jack: I'm scared all the time about doing something stupid, but it's only me who makes that choice. No one else.

Sometimes it turns out that the evidence may support the possibility of a certain outcome happening. In other words, the client may be realistic in his or her assessment of a situation. In those instances, the next line of questioning may be about the "helpfulness" of such thoughts (Creed et al., 2011). For instance, let's say a person with weak math skills is about to take a test and has failed math tests in the past. Her thoughts are, "I'm terrible at math. I'm stupid. I'm going to fail." There is a possibility that she may not do well on the test, but repeating these thoughts to herself will not help matters; it will only increase her anxiety, which may cloud any math ability she does have. Therefore, in these instances, the person can be asked, "How helpful is it to keep saying that to yourself over and over again? Will it make you perform any better?" Most people will deduce that it will not and may be willing to proceed with the process of cognitive restructuring.

TABLE 5.5: Generating Alternative Perspectives (Reframing)

Ask, "What's another way of seeing this?" "What's the silver lining?"

Ask about the perspective of other people in the client's life: "How would your mother say you have been doing since you returned home? What would your girlfriend say about your drinking now?" (deJong & Berg, 2012). Using questions such as these will challenge clients to appraise themselves more realistically through the perceptions of other people.

Ask clients how they would respond to a friend who voiced the same kind of thinking.

Attribution training, presented in Chapter 6, is another way to train clients to generate a new perspective based on theoretical principles.

ALTERNATIVE INTERPRETATIONS OF THE SITUATION

Another way to challenge distorted thinking is to get clients to view the problem from another perspective (McKay, Davis, & Fanning, 2011), one that gives credit for the positive aspects of a situation or behavior. This is also referred to as *reframing*. Table 5.5 outlines ways you can help clients reframe their beliefs and situations.

WORST-CASE SCENARIO

Asking about the client's worst fears attached to the troublesome belief confronts the common cognitive distortion of catastrophizing. In this distortion (outlined with others in Example 5.3, one sees disaster in every situation. A related belief has to do with the inability to handle any suffering or even discomfort.

EXAMPLE 5.3: CHALLENGING UNREALISTIC THOUGHTS

Case Example #1: Nina is a 26-year-old white female who was sexually assaulted by an acquaintance at college.

Social Work Intern: Let's talk about this thought you are having that you will "never have friends again." What would you say supports this?

Nina: I have lost a lot of friends after the assault. Many of my friends are his friends and they really like him despite his reputation as a womanizer. I had to just stop talking to them. They don't know what he actually does to get with all those girls. One time I told two girls in my sorority and when I did they just said, "Well,

(continued)

---

what did you expect?" or "Well, that is just Bobby. I'm sure you are misunderstanding what happened."

Social Work Intern: How did you feel about that?

Nina: I was at first shocked. I mean, I was hesitant to tell people in the first place, and I assumed people would have these kinds of reactions, but for them to have them....I was mortified. So, I just played along like the two girls were probably right just to get out of the conversation, and then I cut them out of my life. And slowly I just started cutting everybody out of my life.

Social Work Intern: That is very disappointing that your friends would act that way. Have you ever told anyone and that wasn't the reaction?

Nina: I told my best friends from high school, and they were extremely supportive. I mean, they just let me get it all out and didn't judge me at all. And now it's been nice because every time I am having a hard time, they understand why and are really there for me.

Social Work Intern: So, these two girlfriends have really offered the support and friendship that you were and still are needing during this time? Anybody else?

Nina: My family. I told my mother first, and then my dad. My dad was upset, but not at me. He was just upset that someone would hurt me like this. But both my parents have been there for me, and I feel like my mom and I have been close in the past year.

Social Work Intern: That is wonderful. So, your parents have been there for you, as well.

Nina: Yeah, I guess....I mean...I just don't have friends like I used to. I lived in the sorority and went to lots of parties and always had a boyfriend. Now I have a hard time relating to people. My group of friends has gone from 100 to 10 in just 3 years.

Social Work Intern: Of these 10 friends, how many of them do you feel you can open up to about the assault?

Nina: Oh, all of them. I mean, I just don't want to waste my time with people who are going to blame me and not hear my side of the story.

Social Work Intern: So, if I am hearing you correctly, it sounds like your group of friends has transformed from quantity to quality.

Nina: Yeah.

Social Work Intern: It is a big change to go through, but it sounds like the people you are surrounding yourself with really have to be of quality and not, as you put it, a waste of your time.

Nina: Yeah, and it's hard because I used to have lots of friends, but looking back on those friendships I realize how superficial they all were.

Social Work Intern: Let's go back to our original thought. The thought that you "will never have friends again." Do you still believe this to be true?

Nina: No.

(continued)

Social Work Intern: What could we change this thought to?

Nina: My group of friend has lessened in number, but has grown in support and love for me as I am.

Case Example #2: This case involves the older women whose depression prevented her from accessing her meal delivery.

Social Work Intern: Let's start thinking about the things that make you think that no one is helping you. The first thing I'll write down is that your friend isn't helping you right now. What else makes you believe that no one is helping you?

Client: Well, I just feel all alone. I mean, I live alone and I have a lot of problems to deal with. I have to take my medication every day. I have to take care of myself every day—take a shower, get dressed, make meals, answer the door when my lunch comes. I have to call the eye doctor and deal with him, because my glasses cost too much and I can't pay him.

Social Work Intern: So you live alone and you feel alone, because of all these things that you have to deal with. Some of it is daily stuff, and some of it is new stuff, like dealing with the eye doctor about your glasses. Does anything else make you feel like no one is helping you?

Client: I had a case manager, but I don't any more. It would be better if she was back and could help me with things. And before that I used to live in an assisted facility, but now I'm on my own here. I don't really want to go back there. They were always telling me what to do and making me take my meds even if I didn't like the side effects. But at least they were there.

Social Work Intern: I can see why you would believe that no one is helping you—you have a lot of responsibilities that you have to manage. Now, these things are all true, but let's think if there are any areas where you might be getting help, even a little bit of help.

Client: Well, I already said my friend helps me sometimes, just not right now. She usually pays for my groceries, but she didn't this month. There are the volunteers who bring me my lunches.

Social Work Intern: Okay, so your friend sometimes helps you by paying for your groceries, and there are volunteers who bring you lunches. Anything else?

Client: My friend also helped pay for part of my glasses, although that's why she didn't pay for my groceries. She said she couldn't afford the groceries after the glasses.

Social Work Intern: So she usually helps you with groceries, but instead this month she helped you pay for part of your glasses. Anything else?

Client: Well, you're here and DHS (Department of Human Services) is coming soon. They might be able to help me more. Maybe they can get me another case manager for a while.

(continued)

> **Social Work Intern:** All right. Your friend sometimes helps you pay for your groceries, and she paid for part of your glasses; volunteers bring you lunch each day; I'm here trying to help; and DHS is coming soon to see how they might be able to help. Is there anything else, anyone else you can think of who is helping you now?
>
> **Client:** [Pauses to think.] No, I think that's it.
>
> **Social Work Intern:** What I see here [showing the two lists to the client] is some ways in which you think and feel that you are not getting help, but on this other side I see some people who are helping you at least a little. If we go back to what you told me, that no one is helping you, what do you think now after looking at this list?
>
> **Client:** I guess that some people ARE helping me. It's not a lot, I still have to do most of my stuff on my own, but some people are helping me with a few things. I mean, I could think about if there are any ways I'm getting help, instead of just thinking about the areas where I'm not getting help.
>
> **Social Work Intern:** I think that's a great plan.

In getting people to identify the worst-case scenario, they may see that the chance of it ever happening is slim, or at least as not as dire as they imagine (McKay et al., 2011). Asking about the worst-case scenario can also help clients consider ways to cope if indeed the worst fear were realized. The social worker might then train the client on coping skills or developing another plan. For example, a social work student worked with a mother who was scared about telling her daughter about her HIV status. To the question "What's the worst that can happen?" Yolanda said that her daughter could tell her friends at school and they could start teasing her daughter. Since this was certainly a possibility, plans were discussed for how her daughter could keep this information private from her friends.

Another way to take the worst-case scenario is to exaggerate the situation to the point of absurdity: "So there you are, having fainted away in front of everyone from anxiety, then what happens?" Humor is often the response to such absurdity, which acts to diffuse some of the intensity of the thoughts.

POINT-COUNTERPOINT

Another way to work with client distortions involves using point-counterpoint. In this technique, the costs and benefits to the client for maintaining certain attitudes are considered (Young, Klosko, & Weishaar, 2003). By partaking in this exercise, clients begin to get a sense that beliefs and cognitions are not as fixed as they once thought, and the very process of exploring beliefs allows their thinking to become more flexible. Example 5.4 shows the results of using point-counterpoint with a client.

EXAMPLE 5.4: POINT-COUNTERPOINT WITH A CLIENT

Kim, a white woman in her mid-20s who cut her arms when distressed, said she realized that she had a belief that she couldn't trust people, that they would disappoint her. She said that the main advantage of the belief was that she remained protected; she didn't have to make herself vulnerable. Another advantage of this belief was that she didn't have to go through the hard work of change. On the disadvantages side, Kim said she had lost out on possibilities for friendship and support because of this belief. She spent a lot of time alone and feeling isolated and disconnected. At the end of the point-counterpoint, Kim was interested in learning how to set up a support network so she wouldn't be relying on only one person whom she was afraid would disappoint. She was also motivated to learn how to identify her needs and communicate them more directly.

DIDACTIC TEACHING AND PSYCHOEDUCATION

Didactic teaching means providing people with the information that will reassure them and will help them find ways to handle their realistic concerns. They are taught how to tease these apart from distorted thinking that is unhelpful to their well-being and functioning (Bandura, 1977).

The assumption is that knowledge (cognitive understanding) of an issue affects the way people feel and behave. For instance, psychoeducation is a common intervention with those who have a mental health issue, such as bipolar disorder. They may learn that people with bipolar disorder may experience certain symptoms; there may be common risk and protective factors influencing the occurrence of the disorder and its eventual outcome; and treatments have been identified. Understanding of the disorder is believed to not only reassure clients but also help them have realistic expectations and provide impetus for behaviors, such as taking medication and keeping a regular schedule. Psychoeducation and delivering education in a collaborative way is the topic of Chapter 10.

EMPIRICAL INVESTIGATIONS

Another way to refute beliefs is to set up experiments to test the extent to which they are irrational. For instance, a person who believes he is unable to relate to others unless he has been drinking can experience a social situation alcohol-free and see realistically what that is like. A person who is afraid that if she goes to school she will be laughed at can observe whether this is indeed the case. By not having the feared outcome occur, the belief may start to lose some of its intensity.

SUBSTITUTING THE THOUGHTS

The final step in cognitive restructuring is to substitute the distorted beliefs with more functional thinking (see Example 5.5).

EXAMPLE 5.5: EXAMPLE OF SUBSTITUTING THOUGHTS

Case Example #1: The elderly woman whose self-defeating thoughts seem to obstruct her ability to access her free meal delivery.

Social Work Intern: Let's see if there's something we can do about this message inside your head that says you're useless. Right now that's a message you're telling yourself, and it's painful, and it doesn't help you get out of bed. What else can you tell yourself that might help you?

Client: I don't know. When I'm like that, I just don't have enough energy.

Social Work Intern: It's hard to think of anything that would help even a small bit?

Client: [Thinking.] Well, I could tell myself that I can go back to bed after I get the meal.

Social Work Intern: That's a good one. I'm going to write that down. [Writes it down on a pad of paper.] What else could you say to yourself?

Client: Maybe I could get out of bed and get the meal, if I try.

Social Work Intern: Okay, that's good, too. [Writes it down.] Do you feel useless all the time?

Client: No, not when I have enough energy and I'm getting things done.

Social Work Intern: So what could you say to yourself when your energy is low, and you're having trouble getting out of bed?

Client: I could tell myself that I'm not always useless; sometimes I can do things.

Social Work Intern: Would you be comfortable if you said that you are not useless? Or would that be too much?

(continued)

> **Client:** I guess I could say that I'm not being useless, I'm just having a hard time getting up.
>
> **Social Work Intern:** I think that's great. So let me see what we've got. You can tell yourself, "I can go back to bed after I get the meal," and "Maybe I could get out of bed and get the meal, if I try," and "I'm not being useless, I'm just having a hard time."
>
> **Client:** I guess I would say, "I'm not being useless, I'm just having a hard time," then "Maybe I could get out of bed and get the meal, if I try," then "I can go back to bed after I get the meal." Then I think I would say, "I'm not being useless, I'm just having a hard time" again. I'll feel silly, saying these things.
>
> **Social Work Intern:** You don't have to say them to anyone else. You don't have to show the list to anyone, or tell them that you're saying new things to yourself. This is just for you, so no one else needs to know. Do you think you'd feel comfortable just practicing these on your own?
>
> **Client:** I could try.
>
> **Social Work Intern:** Good. Try reading these to yourself, and if you want, you can keep them by your bed so you can read them if you're having trouble getting your next meal.

KNOWING WHEN TO USE COGNITIVE RESTRUCTURING

Part of learning about CBT is knowing when to employ what techniques at what point in the change process. Chapter 9 discusses the Transtheoretical Stages of Change Model and the place of CBT within a client's readiness to change. Appendix B presents treatment manuals that can also help guide your choices. Here, we center directly on the appropriateness of cognitive restructuring in terms of certain client problems and populations. Most important to emphasize is that cognitive restructuring should not be used as a way of "assisting people to accommodate to what may fundamentally be unjust or otherwise problematic environments and circumstances" (Cormier et al., 2009, p. 385). For example, if a client's home is infested or is in disrepair, then you wouldn't work with the client to not be bothered by the situation. You would work at the environmental level to attend to these conditions, perhaps also helping the client in her ability to assertively communicate and be an advocate for herself.

Exercise 5.2 offers guidelines to help you determine when cognitive restructuring may be the technique of choice. Students are then asked to think about each guideline and come up with an example that takes it into account.

EXERCISE 5.2: GUIDELINES FOR WHEN TO USE COGNITIVE RESTRUCTURING

Exercise Instructions: After reading the examples, have a class discussion about the types of cases that would be relevant from your practice settings.

When to Use Cognitive Restructuring	Example	Student Example
People are distressed by painful emotions or commit behaviors that are detrimental to themselves or to others. Chances are, a belief may underlie these emotions or actions.	A woman described that, after breaking up with an abusive boyfriend, her stomach became upset, she started shaking, and she felt compelled to call him back. When asked, "What was going through your mind?" the client reported that she was thinking, "What am I going to do? I'm never going to be able to make it without him. I can't do it. Without him, I have nothing." These thoughts were appropriate to target for restructuring, as they were preventing her from making a clean break from an abusive boyfriend.	
A client uses "absolutist" language—"never," "always," "should," and "have to."	"I'm *never* going to be able to make it without him."	
In the midst of other work you're doing with a client, the client's beliefs seem to be a barrier to change.	An intern working with a man with paranoid schizophrenia on assertiveness was having difficulty until she started exploring his fear of being considered "stupid" by others if he voiced his opinion or preference.	

Following are considerations in implementing CBT with certain populations or people with particular problems, along with suggestions for adaptations.

PEOPLE WITH HALLUCINATIONS AND DELUSIONS

Cognitive restructuring requires the ability to think in abstract and logical ways. When individuals are actively psychotic, they often cannot distance themselves from their symptoms sufficiently to consider other ways of thinking. Therefore, cognitive restructuring should only be used when the client is stabilized and only in areas where thinking is relatively stable.

PEOPLE WITH COGNITIVE DISABILITIES

In general, restructuring techniques are best suited for those with the cognitive abilities required to process and understand the approach. The majority of people with a cognitive disability are in the mild category, and therefore, may be able to benefit, depending on their other supports. A few studies have looked at CBT for this population (see Taylor, Lindsay, & Willner, 2008, for a review), and there is preliminary evidence of effectiveness. The more cognitively-oriented techniques have usually focused on increasing helpful self-statements and self-management rather than recognizing distorted thinking and restructuring it.

CHILDREN

In reviews of more cognitively oriented interventions for children, they seem to work less well in children under the age of 11 (Watanabe et al., 2007). Cognitive interventions generally require the stage of formal operations, as such interventions demand consequential and hypothetical thinking and meta-cognition, the ability to think about thoughts, and the ability to manipulate them. Cognitive abilities should be sufficiently developed to enable shifts in thinking about the past and the future, to follow logic, and to grasp abstractions. Also, clients may be delayed cognitively or have learning disorders, which may further inhibit their ability to benefit from cognitive interventions (Shelby & Berk, 2009). Therefore, methods may have to be adapted through use of artwork, analogies, and puppets (e.g., Webster-Stratton, 2012). Some ideas for modifications with children are listed in Table 5.6.

RELIGIOUS GROUPS

Many of our clients, especially those who are ethnically diverse, identify with the Christian faith. Some recent Christian writers, notably Joel Osteen and Joyce Meyers, have adapted the CBT focus on the importance of a person's thought life for how they feel and behave, but here the replacement thoughts and self-talk statements are often taken from the Bible.

TABLE 5.6: Modifications for Children*

Modifications	Explanations
Motoric and kinesthetic games teach the relationship between thoughts, feelings, and behaviors	Yarn, dominoes
Interactive metaphors or stories	"Good coach/bad coach"
Guess what I'm thinking	Act out different scenarios and have child guess self-talk
Thought bubble activity	Child fills in possible thoughts for different cartoons
Dry erase board to write out thoughts	Child can obtain a visual understanding
Note cards with thought-challenging questions	Child can have visual understanding and can take note cards as physical reminder to review

*Source: Knell and Dasari (2009)

Reciting relevant scriptural passages can bring comfort, can help the client connect to a positive belief system, and can develop some meaning in suffering.

Practice in using cognitive restructuring in certain client populations is provided in Exercise 5.3.

EXERCISE 5.3: COGNITIVE RESTRUCTURING IN CLIENT POPULATIONS

What is your client population? Select a client and his or her presenting problem that may benefit from cognitive restructuring. Write down the title of a manual from Appendix A or Appendix B that seems to fit the nature of the problem. Discuss how you might adapt it to make it relevant.

_____

_____

_____

_____

_____

If there is no manual for your population or problem, what adaptations can you make for cognitive restructuring to be relevant?

_____

_____

_____

_____

_____

CONCLUSION

This chapter has introduced cognitive interventions that focus on the role of people's beliefs and thoughts and how these can be changed in order to impact distress and problems in functioning. The process of cognitive restructuring was detailed, along with accompanying examples and exercises to further familiarize you with the techniques. The variety of ways in which practitioners can help people identify and replace their faulty cognitive patterns were also outlined in this chapter.

TEST YOUR SKILLS EXERCISE 5.1: COGNITIVE RESTRUCTURING

Case Example #1: Cynthia Jones is a 67-year-old white woman whose husband died a few years ago after a long illness. She has been diagnosed with depression. The intern has been talking to her about attending a senior center which offers leisure programs and services, continued education, and access to community resources, and crafts, but Mrs. Jones has been reluctant to go.

Cynthia: I've been thinking about the Rosewood Center I used to go to. I was able to get out of my house and connect with people who at times liked the same things I did.

Social Work Intern: Being able to surround yourself with people who have similar interests can be a good thing.

Cynthia: Yes, I liked it, but at times I felt guilty.

Social Work Intern: What do you think caused you to feel that way?

Cynthia: I wasn't really helping anyone. I'm so used to helping, helping, helping. I almost felt like I should have been helping my friends who are sick instead of being at the center and taking time for myself. I felt as if I wasn't doing any good. I feel selfish because I'm so used to helping. I kind of feel like it is my identity.

What belief would you target here?

_____

_____

_____

Case Example #2: A social work intern is placed at an alternative high school for students at risk of dropping out. One of her clients, Jason, a 17-year-old African-American, has made good use of his time at the alternative school and is going from poor grades and excessive absence to making a post-secondary plan. He wants to attend a 4-year university and needs to write an essay for the applications. The intern had been checking in with him the last couple of times, but he can't seem to get down to the task of writing the essay.

Social Work Intern: How are you today?

Jason: I'm fine, but I didn't work on the essay.

Social Work Intern: What's going on?

Jason: It's hard, and I just don't know what to write about or where to begin. I sit there and can't come up with anything.

(continued)

Social Work Intern: Getting started can be the most difficult part. What are you telling yourself when you're sitting there trying to type?

Jason: I don't know.

Social Work Intern: Let's try something. Close your eyes and picture yourself at your computer. (Client does so.) What thoughts come to mind when you're about to type?

Jason: I'm a terrible writer.... It's not going to be good enough.... What's the point? (He opens his eyes.) I don't know, I guess that kind of stuff.

What process for cognitive restructuring was the intern doing here? Would you make any changes to what she has done?

_____

_____

_____

Social Work Intern: You have these thoughts, and then you're unable to start writing the essay.

Jason: Yeah.

Social Work Intern: Jason, I want to talk to you about how our thoughts are connected to our feelings and actions. Let me draw a diagram for you to show this better. (Draws triangle connecting these). Do you see how these connect?

Jason: Yes.

Social Work Intern: Okay, so when you try to write the essay, you feel discouraged and hopeless and then you start thinking you're a bad writer and it's not going to be good enough. That's what causes the writing block, and then you don't write the essay.

Jason: Right, then I just give up 'cause it's hard.

What was the process of cognitive restructuring she was doing here? Do you have any suggestions or changes you would make?

_____

_____

_____

Social Work Intern: You get frustrated. Do you mind if we look more into these thoughts you're having to learn more about what's blocking you from writing?

Jason: That's fine.

Social Work Intern: Have you written something in the past that wasn't good?

Jason: Ummm, I'm not sure. I don't write that much.

(continued)

Social Work Intern: So maybe not having a lot of experience scares you a little, but you've never been told you were a bad writer.

Jason: No, I don't think so.

Social Work Intern: What would you say is the worst-case scenario in actually writing the essay?

Jason: (Pause) I guess that you wouldn't like it.

Social Work Intern: Have I ever not liked something you did?

Jason: I don't think so.

Social Work Intern: Well, I'm honored you want my approval, but honestly, I'm just here to help you.

Jason: I know, I just don't want to look stupid.

Social Work Intern: You're worried that your lack of experience may cause you not to write the best essay. This is just a first draft. Nothing you write is going to make you look stupid. What do you think makes you so worried about not being able to write this essay?

Jason: That I have to write about myself.

Social Work Intern: You're concerned with writing about yourself and that it might not be good enough.

Jason: Yeah, colleges aren't going to want to accept me.

Social Work Intern: Have you ever applied to college?

Jason: No.

Social Work Intern: So, you've never been rejected from college?

Jason: No.

Social Work Intern: Then you don't really know that they won't accept you. Tell me about a time recently when you were accepted into something.

Jason: I'm not sure.

Social Work Intern: Tell me about how you got into the alternative school.

Jason: I was failing, and I knew it would help me catch up.

Social Work Intern: So, you knew that by coming here you could do better and graduate with your class. How did you actually get into this program?

Jason: My guidance counselor referred me and then my mom came and we talked about it.

Social Work Intern: Do you think you would have gotten in here if you just walked into this office and asked?

Jason: Probably not.

Social Work Intern: Do you think that having a guidance counselor refer you and you and your mom deciding it was a good idea, and her enrolling you is how you got *accepted*?

Jason: I didn't think about it that way.

(continued)

Social Work Intern: What improvements have you made since coming here?

Jason: My grades have gone up and I'm finishing classes.

Social Work Intern: It sounds like you've made some pretty important changes in the last year. What happened that made you want to improve your grades and get a diploma?

Jason: I knew I wouldn't get anywhere living the life I was living. I wanted to make something of myself.

Social Work Intern: You knew you weren't making the best decisions and needed to do something about it.

Jason: Right.

Social Work Intern: May I give you an idea?

Jason: Sure.

Social Work Intern: That sounds like a great way to start your essay about why you want to go to college. You've had great academic achievements over the last year, and it was because you motivated yourself to do it. I think that will help you stand out to college admissions.

Jason: Yeah, I guess so. I just need to get my mind right and actually do it.

Social Work Intern: Exactly, and you have more to write about than you may realize. Remember, this is only a first draft and you have me, the college advisor, and teachers to help you finalize it. No matter what you write on your first draft, it's not going to prevent you from going to college.

What processes did the intern use to determine the validity of the student's thoughts?

_____

_____

_____

Case Example #3: George is a 24-year-old African-American male. George has a limited support system and lives with his grandmother, as his mother died when he was young. George has been seeing the intern for case management and employment assistance. He has been discouraged about his lack of progress in gaining employment.

Social Work Intern: George, when you first started meeting with me, you said that your main goal was to find a job, so that's what we've been working on. I know a lot of things have been going on in your life recently, so I wanted to give you a chance to re-evaluate your plan. Is finding a job still your main focus?

George: It is, but it seems like no matter what I do and no matter how hard I try, no good comes of it.

(continued)

Social Work Intern: You feel discouraged that nothing has come through for you yet.

George: Yeah.

Social Work Intern: When you started looking for a job, did you think it was going to be easy or that you'd be hired immediately?

George: No, I knew it would be hard, but everything I do ends up as a failure anyway.

Social Work Intern: What about when you've found jobs in the past, do you consider that a failure?

George: No.

Social Work Intern: It's just discouraging right now because although you've gotten close, the ultimate goal is to have a job, and that still hasn't happened.

George: Yeah.

Social Work Intern: So you've said that you knew finding a job wasn't going to be easy and that it is a process. Do you feel like you haven't made any progress at all since we've been meeting?

George: I don't know.

Social Work Intern: We've been meeting pretty regularly. What would you say we've done?

George: I remember getting my resumé done when I first started coming here.

Social Work Intern: Yeah, what else?

George: Not much.

Social Work Intern: When you went home in between our sessions, did you just sit around and do nothing?

George: No, I'd go check out places that we talked about to try to get a job and put in applications.

Social Work Intern: And when you'd come back to see me, did you come empty-handed?

George: No, I'd bring in information about places I applied to, or we'd fill out an application online. And I did get an interview with that one place. It felt like I was getting really close to being hired.

Social Work Intern: So, you have made progress, and even though it seems like a failure whenever an employer turns you down, we knew from the beginning that that would probably happen a few times. So in a way it takes some little setbacks to continue to make progress and achieve your goal.

George: Yeah, I guess it's just a part of the process. You have to take baby steps. I know that I'm just not gonna get a job right away.

Social Work Intern: When you start thinking about how you're not making any progress, what kind of feelings do you have?

(continued)

George: I'm mostly sad, but I get angry too.

Social Work Intern: What do you usually do when you're sad and angry?

George: I sit in my room, and I don't talk to anybody.

Social Work Intern: Does that make you feel better?

George: Not really.

Social Work Intern: When you get sad and stay in your room, do you ever leave and go job hunt?

George: No, I don't ever really leave my room when I get like that.

Social Work Intern: So things start with you thinking about how you're not making any progress in finding a job. Those thoughts lead to you becoming sad and angry. Then, being sad and angry makes you stay in your room, which actually hurts your chances of finding a job, which is the whole reason you had those thoughts in the first place. Do you see how you can get stuck in a destructive cycle?

George: Yeah, I see that.

Social Work Intern: If you feel yourself start to have those thoughts, what could you try to do instead?

George: I guess I could think about the progress I have made, like the stuff we just talked about.

Social Work Intern: I think that would be a good plan.

George: Okay.

Social Work Intern: You said that things seem to turn out as failures for you. What do you think the worst-case scenario would be if things don't get better?

George: I'd continue to have nothing to show for myself. My grandmother isn't doing very well. If she dies, I would have nothing and I'd be all alone.

Social Work Intern: What do you think would happen to you?

George: I'd have to find someone else to stay with. I might become homeless. I'd just have nothing.

Social Work Intern: Before your mother died, if I asked you what things would be like if she died, what would you have said.

George: Probably the same thing.

Social Work Intern: Then, your mom did die. Were you all alone?

George: No, it was really hard, but that's when I became close with my grandmother.

Social Work Intern: You were just a kid then. Now, that you're older, do you think you would be better or worse at handling a situation like that?

George: Probably better.

Social Work Intern: So, even if things get as bad as they can get, it's still not going to be the worst thing that's ever happened to you.

George: Yeah.

(continued)

Social Work Intern: You haven't given up yet. I would call that a success in its own right. You still want to find a job, and the two main choices you have right now are to give up, which you haven't shown me any signs of, or to keep trying. And keep in mind that we already determined that what you have been doing has been working, it just hasn't paid off yet.

George: Yeah, I guess I don't have any other choice.

What ways of examining the validity of thoughts did the student use? How well did this work?

_____

_____

_____

SECTION FOUR

SKILL-BUILDING

CHAPTER 6

COGNITIVE COPING

This section covers a class of coping techniques that are cognitive in nature, having to do with the manipulation of thoughts in order to feel and behave differently and to manage stressful life events more effectively. Again, this does not mean, however, that when you work with people who are impoverished that you want them to accept conditions that are oppressive or discriminatory.

That being said, cognitive coping techniques are helpful in those circumstances that a client may not be able to change. In those cases, the client can only change his or her perspective to accept the circumstances and perhaps derive meaning from the situation. For instance, I have worked in several divorce situations in which the child is court-ordered to have visitation with a parent who may not be providing the child an appropriate environment. If there is no altering of these circumstances through working with either parent or going through legal venues, I help the child develop ways to cope with the situation.

SELF-TALK

Self-talk, broadly speaking, is a means of giving clients an internal cognitive framework for instructing themselves in how to cope effectively with problem situations (Meichenbaum, 1999). It is based in part on the premise that many people as a matter of course engage in internal speech, giving themselves "pep talks" to prepare for certain challenges. Further, when people find themselves in difficult situations, those that evoke tension or other negative emotions, their thinking may become confused, and their ability to cope diminishes.

Clients need to be trained in self-talk skills so that they can equip themselves to perform the strategies outlined in Table 6.1. See Example 6.1 and Exercise 6.1 for practice using self-talk with a client.

TABLE 6.1: Self-Talk Strategies

Guideline	Example
Approach stressful situations	"I'll be okay—this is just a problem to be solved," "It's okay to feel discouraged, but I can deal with this."
Manage the event as the client is experiencing it, through coping statements	"I can do this" "I'm doing just fine" "I'm nervous, but I can handle this" "It'll be over soon"
Praise oneself afterward	"You did a good job," "That was tough, but you stuck to it," "Next time it'll be even easier."

EXAMPLE 6.1: SELF-TALK

Paula, a ventilator patient with Lou Gehrig's disease, said that she sometimes had difficulty breathing and would grow panicky while waiting for the respiratory therapist to assist her. When the social worker asked her what thoughts ran through her mind, Paula described statements such as "they're never going to get here" and "I can't breathe, I can't breathe." The social worker then modeled some alternative self-coping statements that Paula could use instead: "I know the therapist is on his way, he always comes," and "I can breathe, I am breathing now, and I will continue to breathe." Next, the social worker had Paula repeat the coping statements. The social worker also modeled self-reinforcement statements for Paula: "I am coping with this situation," "I am doing a good job," "I am getting better at this," and "That wasn't so bad." Each time, Paula repeated the statements after the social worker.

The social worker then asked Paula to talk about another event that caused her anxiety. She responded that she often felt anxious while she was waiting for the nurse to come and clean her after a bowel movement. The loss of control of body functions was especially difficult for Paula. She would tend to blame herself while she waited, saying things like "If I hadn't gone to the bathroom in the first place, this wouldn't have happened, I should have known this was coming." These types of statements only increased her sense of being upset.

The social worker modeled coping statements that she asked Paula to repeat aloud: "I really can't help it when it happens. It's just an unfortunate part of having this disease. The nurse will be here just a soon as she can." "It can't be helped, I am going to cope with this situation." "Stay calm for just a little longer, I can do this." The social worker then asked her to reinforced herself afterward: "That wasn't so bad, I'll do even better next time."

EXERCISE 6.1: SELF-TALK DURING A STRESSFUL SITUATION

Exercise Instructions: Consider a client with whom you are working that is having difficulty facing a stressful event. Breaking down the stressful event into the following three categories, come up with self-talk that would be appropriate and helpful to the situation.

Times to Use Self-Talk	Client Response
Approach stressful situation	
Manage the event as it's going on	
Praise afterward	

ATTRIBUTION THEORY

Attributional theory posits that the explanation people note for the events in their lives help them manage, control, and master these events. This in turn affects emotional adjustment and coping (Gotlib & Abramson, 1999; White & Barrowclough, 1998). Attributional theory further contends that there are patterns to these attributions that are organized around certain dimensions:

1) The extent to which individuals attribute causes of events to internal (to the individual) or external (outside the individual) factors
2) Whether the factor is an overall global characteristic (i.e., the world is unsafe) or a specific event or behavior (i.e., a hurricane happened)
3) Depending on the theory, the degree to which the event can be controlled (Weiner, 1985) or its stability, whether it will always be there or if it is temporary (Gotlib & Abramson, 1999)

Depression is one area to which attributional theory has been applied. Persons with depression have a habitual tendency toward pessimism by making external, specific, temporary attributions for success and internal, global, and stable explanations for failure (Abramson, Metalsky, & Alloy, 1989), as Table 6.2 presents. In some depression treatment programs, such as self-control therapy for children (Stark, Reynolds, & Kaslow, 1987; Stark, Rouse, & Livingston, 1991), the aim is that clients stop blaming themselves for negative events and instead see them as temporary. This school-based intervention for elementary-age children relies on attribution retraining as part of the intervention so clients can reverse this style of thinking and make more appropriate attributions for events (Stark et al., 1987, 1991).

TABLE 6.2: Attribution Patterns of Pessimism and Depression

Presence of Depression	Explanation for Success	Explanation for Failure
Person with depression	Success is external, specific, and temporary. "I got a good grade because she offered an easy test."	Failure is internal, global, and stable. "I did poorly because I'm stupid."
Person without depression	Success is internal, global, and stable. "I did well because I'm smart."	Failure is external, specific, and temporary. "The teacher graded that test hard."

Along with depression, parenting has also been a domain to which attribution theory has been applied. The attributions that parents give for their children's behavior affect how they behave toward their children (White & Barrowclough, 1998). Reviews of research have indicated that mothers of children without problems employ a positive attributional bias for their children. They view prosocial behavior by their children as being due to internal characteristics of the child that are stable in nature, whereas deviant behavior is seen as situational and temporary (Freeman, Johnston, & Barth, 1997). These parents typically believe they have control over parenting interactions because of parental competence and skills.

Mothers of children with behavior problems and parents who maltreat their children display an opposite pattern: they explain their children's deviance as being due to dispositional and stable causes within their children (Wakefield, Kirk, Hsieh & Pottick, 1999). As a result, these mothers downplay their parenting practices as determining their children's behavior. Because they do not believe they have control in parenting their children, apathy, depression, and hopelessness may follow (Gotlib & Abramson, 1999), and they may not comply with treatment or follow through with intervention, believing it will not work (Corcoran & Ivery, 2004).

Therefore, social workers should attend to parental statements about child misbehavior and reframe the reasons parents offer involving internal and dispositional qualities of the child. For example, a mother might say, "These kids are just hard-headed like their father. That's why they won't listen." The social worker can then reframe the attribution, offering another perspective. In this example, the social worker can reframe the parent's attribution of her children as "hard headed" (a fixed and inherent quality of her children that has been inherited from their father) to one involving more temporary and changeable circumstances: "I wonder if they are just tired at that time of night and are cranky as a result." Another way to reframe parents' attributions of their children's negative behaviors as being due to dispositional qualities is by offering an alternative view that is compatible with the available data (D'Zurilla & Nezu, 2010): "It seems like your child is more likely to push the other kids when the classroom is full, and the children have to share a lot." Yet another method is to ask parents when they give an attribution for their child acting out to come up with other possible reasons. In this way, they are enabled to see their child from different perspectives. Exercise 6.2 provides practice in retraining attributions.

FOCUS ON STRENGTHS-BASED THINKING

In the last chapter, cognitive restructuring was discussed as a process by which people identify thoughts that are irrational and unhelpful, question their validity, and substitute these thoughts. However, looking for negative thinking and arguing against it may draw too much attention to the problem, if examined from a strengths-based perspective. Instead, there can be a process of locating thoughts and beliefs that are already working well for the individual. In his writings on cognitions, Martin Seligman, who started the field of positive psychology, claims that having positive thoughts is more important than decreasing negative thoughts. In fact, he suggests that people should have twice the number of positive thoughts as negative ones (Seligman, 2011). Some ideas for how to work with clients from this perspective are offered in Table 6.3.

Solution-focused writers have also produced some ideas about how to identify positive thoughts, through coping questions (e.g., deJong & Berg, 2012). When people talk about their problems and suffering, they need to be validated. Coping questions were designed to achieve this; they also act as a bridge to help people get in touch with their strengths. An example of such questions is as follows: "This sounds very hard. What are you telling yourself to manage this? What are you telling yourself to keep going?"

Exercise 6.3 provides examples of unhelpful and positive thoughts, as well as practice in identifying these in a client.

TABLE 6.3: Working with Thoughts from a Strengths-Based Perspective

People can be asked to pay attention to the thoughts that serve them well. What are they telling themselves during stressful circumstances that are helpful?

Have people count the number of positive thoughts they have and then try to increase the percentage, perhaps by 10% each week.

Write down negative thoughts, but then find two alternative positive thoughts to counteract each one (see Example 6.2).

EXERCISE 6.3: IDENTIFYING UNHELPFUL THOUGHTS AND REPLACING WITH TWO HELPFUL THOUGHTS

Unhelpful Thoughts	Helpful and Positive Thoughts
Samantha, a single white female suffering from depression, mentions that a coworker said she looked tired.	"I enjoyed staying up last night to watch that movie, even though I'm a bit tired today."
Her unhelpful thought was: "I must look really ugly."	"My coworker sounded concerned about me."
Marissa, a white 15-year-old who has a problem with "cutting," identified that one of her triggers was when a boy she liked didn't pay attention to her.	"I'm looking forward to talking to my best friend on the phone after school."
Her thoughts were: "The day is ruined. What is wrong with me?"	"I am in control of the way I feel."

Your client example:

THOUGHT-STOPPING

Sometimes, people seem unable to stop having certain distorted thought patterns that are not serving their interests. To interrupt these negative patterns, thought-stopping can be taught.

When alone and thinking negatively, clients are instructed to yell "STOP" as loudly as possible and to then say, "I won't think about that any more." They are told to gradually change from yelling to thinking "Stop" so that the technique can be used in public. See Example 6.2.

EXAMPLE 6.2: THOUGHT-STOPPING

Case Example #1: Cheryl, an African-American 18-year old, has been living with a foster family, Mr. and Mrs. Johnson, for the last two years. Also in the household is the Johnson's biological grandchild, Kenny, of whom they have custody. Since Cheryl has graduated from high school, her foster parents expect her to get a job, but she has not been looking. Cheryl is also not doing her chores or complying with the Johnsons' house rules.

After the social work student worked with Cheryl, Cheryl had a lot of understanding about the connection between the way she thought ("They're going to kick me out") and her feelings (anger at them) and behaviors (wanting to get back at them and not get a job). Cheryl also realized, "Being kicked out is just what I'm used to from my past foster parents. My real mom—that's what she did, too. She kicked me out of the house when I was really young." But then she went on to say, "I just don't know how to stop having these thoughts that they don't love me and want me to leave."

The intern introduced the technique of *thought-stopping* to Cheryl, and explained that every time she thought about the Johnsons kicking her out, about them not loving her, or any other negative thought that was not realistic or based on facts or evidence, that she should use the technique. They practiced this in Cheryl's session, with Cheryl first saying "Stop!" very loudly when she had the negative thoughts and then saying it to herself.

Case Example #2: David, an 11-year-old African-American boy was physically and emotionally abused by his uncle while his mother was in treatment. For the thought-stopping unit, the intern explained that this was a way for him to stop himself from being preoccupied with the abuse by his uncle and with his negative messages.

> **David:** So, you're going to make me stop my thoughts?
> **Social Worker:** Yes, think about what happened with your uncle.
> **David:** (Closes his eyes, remains silent).
> **Social Worker:** (CLAPS HANDS LOUDLY)
> **David:** Ah! You scared me.
> **Social Worker:** But you stopped thinking about it, right?
> **David:** Whoa, yeah, I did.

David and the clinician then discussed ways this could be done without her assistance. She explained a few options: a rubber band on his wrist, saying "go away" out loud, or saying it inside his head. David stated that he did not want his peers to hear him talking to himself because it was "not a good look" and agreed to stop

(continued)

his thoughts in his own head. The clinician explained that he could then replace the thought with the thought of his grandmother's backyard or a similar positive thought, such as sharing a home-cooked meal with his large family. David was worried about getting stuck in his thoughts and forgetting to remind himself, and the clinician promised to continue to review the strategy with him.

CONCLUSION

This chapter has focused on the development of cognitive ways that clients can cope with challenges. Generally, these are reserved for situations in which one's perspective must change because the environment will not. That is not to say we shouldn't work very hard to help clients with their environmental stressors and to build their capacity to influence them. At the same time, a new cognitive perspective may aid a client in adjusting well to hardships.

CHAPTER 7

BEHAVIORAL COPING SKILLS

This chapter focuses on behavioral coping skills that the social worker can help clients develop. Coping skills, broadly defined, are tools that help individuals manage and negotiate stressful events. By being better able to manage stressors, individuals will perceive themselves as more competent; increased confidence and competence will lead to further positive steps and more reinforcement from the environment as a result.

AVOIDANCE

One way people can learn to manage difficult events is to make the necessary preparations to avoid stressful or negative situations. For instance, if spending time with a particular person always makes one feel bad about oneself later, one strategy may be to avoid spending time with that person. If a person has been abusive in the past, he might be coached on how to avoid finding himself in an ex-girlfriend's neighborhood.

A distinction must be made between avoidance as a healthy coping strategy and avoidance used in a harmful way. Healthy avoidance usually involves the people, places, and things involved in a problem behavior. However, using avoidance to ignore responsibilities and relationships can be detrimental to the person. Indeed, avoidance as a habitual coping mechanism has been implicated in many mental health problems (Holahan, Moos, Holahan, Brennan, & Schutte, 2005). When problems are handled by simply pretending they don't exist, one doesn't learn how to deal with the stressor, and then there are additional consequences for not handling the problem. For example, a student who decides she doesn't like research avoids producing a research project or studying for a test. She then gets a poor grade and may feel badly about herself.

While avoidance can be unhealthy, distraction has been found to be a helpful way to cope with negative feelings. For example, Nolen-Hoeksema (2002) discusses gender differences in coping between males and females to explain the higher rates of depression in females. She suggests that rumination is a common pattern found in women, whereas men use distraction and problem-solving if they experience distressing feelings.

Because it can sometimes be difficult to tell the difference between healthy distraction and avoidance, some patterns to keep in mind are the pervasiveness and the temporal nature of the strategy. Is it used on a short-term basis until a bad mood passes, or is it a strategy that is employed throughout the day at the expense of other responsibilities that should be filled? Exercise 7.1 provides practice in identifying healthy and unhealthy uses of avoidance.

RELAXATION TRAINING

Relaxation training is taught to people to reduce their anxiety and tension. Although relaxation training is described here on its own, it is typically paired with some other technique. Recall that exposure is used as the major treatment for anxiety disorders (see Chapter 2). To briefly summarize here, exposure allows gradated contact over time with the feared object in order to dissipate anxiety. Relaxation training is always paired with exposure, so that the person is thoroughly versed on how to induce relaxation in session and for consistent out-of-session homework. The person has to be able to relax on cue, to counteract the feelings of anxiety that surface during exposure of the feared object. In this way, the person is able to manage and move past the physiological tension.

TABLE 7.1: Relaxation Methods

Technique	Explanation
Jacobsen technique	The Jacobson technique involves progressive muscle relaxation in which an individual is instructed to tense the muscles in his or her arms and hands, then relax them. Next the individual is asked to tense his or her face and forehead, followed by the shoulders, back, chest, and stomach, then legs. After tensing each muscle group, the person is told to relax and is given instructions on abdominal breathing and the effect of breathing deeply on relaxation. Approximately seven seconds are devoted to tensing each muscle group and about seven seconds are devoted to relaxing the muscle group.
Benson technique	The Benson technique is considered a less conspicuous way to relax (Rohde et al., 2005). For this procedure, the person is instructed to choose a word or phrase to repeat to him- or herself. Some possibilities include the words "one," "relax," "om," and "peace." The person is told to sit quietly with eyes closed, focusing on breathing, saying the chosen word while breathing out and progressively relaxing muscle groups. It is recommended that the person do this for 10 to 20 minutes and then sit quietly for a few minutes.

There are two different relaxation methods: the Jacobson technique and the Benson technique, described in more detail in Table 7.1. An abundance of Internet resources also now exist on these methods, as well as many audio recordings; Table 7.2 lists some excellent sources.

In either of these two practices, people typically experience difficulties, such as distracting thoughts, external distractions, or physical reactions and sensations. Attention from distracting thoughts is redirected by focusing on breathing or repeating a special word or phrase, and making sure that the relaxation is being done in a quiet place at a quiet time. Clients are expected to practice relaxation at least once a day so they can become adept at inducing a relaxed state at will. By practicing, they will also see the benefits of relaxation for reducing stress and of feeling increased well-being.

TABLE 7.2: Website Resources for Relaxation Methods

Relaxation processes are of three different varieties. Each is listed here with websites where you can find examples

Deep breathing	http://www.drweil.com/drw/u/ART00521/three-breathing-exercises.html
	http://www.webmd.com/balance/stress-managemefnt/stress-management-breathing-exercises-for-relaxation
Progressive muscle relaxation	http://www.webmd.com/balance/stress-management/stress-management-doing-progressive-muscle-relaxation
	http://www.the-guided-meditation-site.com/progressive-muscle-relaxation-script.html
Visualization	http://www.webmd.com/balance/stress-management/stress-management-doing-guided-imagery-to-relax
	http://www.the-guided-meditation-site.com/guided-meditation-script.html
	http://www.exploremeditation.com/guided-imagery-scripts/
Meditation	http://nccam.nih.gov/health/meditation/overview.htm

For some clients, relaxation training may feel foreign or artificial, even after they have tried it. Fortunately, there are many alternative ways to relax and reduce tension.

VISUALIZATION

Visualization is one such option. Recall in Chapter 6 the client Paula, who had been diagnosed with Lou Gehrig's disease and had lost control of her muscle function as a result. Therefore, relaxation training was not feasible for her. Instead, she visualized happy moments with her children, which gave her a sense of well-being when she faced difficult situations and procedures associated with her disease. See also Example 7.1.

SELF-CARE ACTIVITIES

Relaxation training can also be considered more broadly as any activity that reduces tension and induces a feeling of relaxation and well-being in a client. "Self-care" activities, in general, fall under this category. Considered this way, clients often call upon a number of activities that are pleasant and enjoyable, such as gardening, craft making, talking on the phone to friends, surfing on the Internet, going out to eat, or taking hot baths or showers, among others. You may have to help clients problem-solve about activities they find to be relaxing. (The process of problem-solving is detailed later in this chapter.)

EXAMPLE 7.1: VISUALIZATION AS A RELAXATION TOOL

Recall the case example of Ms. Jackson in Chapter 5, the mother of two children with sickle cell anemia. Because she did not have many ways to reduce tension, the social work intern asked Ms. Jackson if she wanted to learn about visualization. Ms. Jackson had heard of the technique before: "I think that's what a psychologist once taught my youngest daughter to do when she was in pain. Some kind of story telling or something. You can tell me more about it."

The social work intern asked Ms. Jackson to identify a place that was relaxing for her (a Caribbean beach), and the intern wrote down the sensory (sight, smell, auditory, tactile) details that Ms. Jackson used to describe the place. The intern told her that in times of anxiety or stress, Ms. Jackson could sit in a relaxing position, close her eyes, and conjure up the place and experience these details. They practiced in the session, and Ms. Jackson reported feeling a sense of relaxation and of being renewed.

MINDFULNESS

Buddhism as a religious philosophy cultivates "mindfulness," which is believed to result from the regular practice of meditation. In this practice, a person is required to sit in a quiet place for a certain period of time and observe his or her breath, focusing the attention on this even as thoughts wander. The idea is to realize that one is not one's thoughts and to go beyond them to reach a state of calm and at peace.

The interest in mindfulness began with a medical doctor, Jon Kabat-Zinn, in the 1970s, who started teaching people with chronic illness to meditate. Over time, mindfulness-based cognitive therapy (http://www.mbct.com) developed as an approach that combines the mindfulness meditation rooted in Buddhist thought and the Western tradition of CBT approaches.

Readers may be more familiar with Linehan's (1993) dialectical behavior therapy for borderline personality disorder. Linehan's rationale for inclusion of a mindfulness component had to do with the intense and often volatile emotions shown by her clients. She used mindfulness as a tool for her clients to enable them to better tolerate their painful emotions; they could become more detached from them, noticing their existence without being compelled to react to others inappropriately or in self-destructive ways. Since then, mindfulness has expanded in popularity to an increasing variety of problems.

Acceptance and commitment therapy (Hayes, Strosahl, & Wilson, 2011) is also part of this third wave of CBT. Its emphasis is on acceptance of situations over which one has no control and cultivating the ability to detach from distress, even as one becomes more tolerant of distressing emotions. More resources on using mindfulness as part of CBT are offered in Appendix B.

ADAPTATIONS FOR CHILDREN

Even for young clients, CBT has a relaxation component. Children who are angered easily, become overwhelmed with stress, or who are anxious, for example, need safe and healthy ways to reduce tension. Adaptations for teaching young people about relaxation are listed in Table 7.3. Example 7.2 illustrates the delivery of such techniques.

TABLE 7.3: **Relaxation Techniques with Children**

Relaxation Technique	Description
Deep breathing	Have the child place stuffed animals on his or her stomach and watch as it rises and falls with deep breaths. Have the child blow bubbles (bubble breathing).
Muscle relaxation	Have the child play a robot (muscular tension) and then spaghetti (loose, relaxed posture) Use yoga poses.

Source: Feindler, 2009; Knell & Dasari, 2009

EXAMPLE 7.2: USING RELAXATION TECHNIQUES

Case Example #1: Keisha is an African-American 12-year-old girl who has been sexually abused by an adult cousin and reports having difficulty sleeping.

Social Work Intern: People who have been sexually abused often feel anxious and can have trouble relaxing, just like you were saying; sometimes they have trouble sleeping.

Keisha: (Nods her head.)

Social Work Intern: Today we are going to work on some relaxation techniques. What do you think about that?

Keisha: That might be okay.

Social Work Intern: So, I have a couple of things we are going to do over the next few weeks. The first is called four-square breathing. And I have two pieces of paper, so that we can do it together, okay?

Keisha: Okay.

Social Work Intern: I also brought some markers that you can use to make this special, just for you. So, on your piece of paper you are going to write "breathe in" on one of the corners.

(Keisha follows the direction.)

Social Work Intern: That looks great. Now on the next corner, I want you to write "hold it," and in the next corner, "breathe out."

Keisha: What do I write in the last corner?

Social Work Intern: Wow, Keisha! You are really moving along. The last corner says "do nothing."

Keisha: What do I do with this?

Social Work Intern: One of the things that works really well when you have anxiety or feel nervous or worried, or even when you're scared, is to practice your breathing to help you calm down. How about we try it together? We are going to go around the square and follow each command for four seconds each.

(Social Work Intern and Keisha participate in the exercise.)

Social Work Intern: Now, let's do it again.

(They repeat it.)

Social Work Intern: How does that feel?

Keisha: It feels a little weird.

Social Work Intern: Yes, it may feel uncomfortable or new for awhile, but I think if you practice every day you may find it helpful with your anxiety. Can you practice it every day or even a couple of times a day? It is even small enough for you to carry with you in your pocket in case you forget.

Keisha: I will try.

(continued)

Social Work Intern: I want you to try it when you are beginning to feel anxious, and let me know how it went next week when you come in.

The next week when they meet, the social work intern asks Keisha about the homework on deep breathing.

Keisha: I forgot to do it most of the week, but I was having a hard time falling asleep Wednesday night, and so I practiced. I am not sure if it worked because I fell asleep!

Social Work Intern: If you fell asleep, that would suggest to me that it worked, right? You were anxious and you couldn't sleep, but after you did the breathing exercise, you fell asleep?

Keisha: Yes, I guess it did work, huh?

Case Example #2: Tana is an 11-year-old white female who was sexually abused by her mother's boyfriend.

Social Work Intern: I brought you these bubbles.
Tana: Oh, I love bubbles.
Social Work Intern: Great! Show me how me how to blow the bubbles.
Tana: You don't know how to blow bubbles?
Social Work Intern: Well, I do, but I want to see how you blow bubbles.
(Tana blows bubbles.)
Social Work Intern: Did you notice how you had to breathe in order to get the most bubbles?
Tana: What do you mean?
Social Work Intern: You have to blow gently, don't you? You can't breathe real fast, like if you were having anxiety, can you?
Tana: (tries) I guess not. I do have to breathe slowly.
Social Work Intern: Let's try to do it together.
(They both blow bubbles.)
Tana: Wow, that is really cool! Can I take them with me?
Social Work Intern: Will you use them when you are feeling anxious?
Tana: Yes, I will.
Social Work Intern: Well, then you can take them!
Tana: Awesome.

Case Example #3: David, age 11, is an African-American boy who was physically and emotionally abused by his uncle. Because he lives in a homeless shelter and does not have much personal space, the skill of visualization as a relaxation technique was substituted for progressive muscle relaxation.

(continued)

Social Work Intern: Tell me about a place where you feel comfortable and safe.

David: My grandma's backyard.

Social Work Intern: Would it be okay if you closed your eyes? Now picture everything about that yard – what you see, smell, and hear.

David: I like it there. My head be quiet there.

Social Work Intern: Remember you told me about your heart racing when you are worried or your fists clenching when you are angry? Closing your eyes and going there will help you calm down.

David: I wish I could always be there.

Social Work Intern: This will help you feel the way you do when you are there.

PROBLEM-SOLVING TRAINING

Individuals often get stuck when faced with stressful situations, not knowing what to do about them. They may avoid the problem altogether. For instance, a woman receives a letter from the electric company stating that her electricity will be turned off for nonpayment. She does nothing, unable to face the problem.

Another common defense against a stressful event is to respond to it as one has before, also unsuccessfully. For example, a child misbehaves and the parent yells, with no effect on the child. People sometimes need to breed flexibility into their problem-solving strategies.

The problem-solving process involves helping clients learn how to produce a variety of potentially effective responses when faced with problem situations (D'Zurilla & Neru, 2010). It includes the following five steps: (1) defining the problem; (2) brainstorming; (3) evaluating the alternatives; (4) choosing and implementing an alternative; and (5) evaluating the implemented option.

DEFINING THE PROBLEM

Although defining the problem sounds like a relatively simple step, there are actually several aspects to a definition that set up a successful problem-solving session.

First, the salient problem must be located. For instance, a client brings up being late for work as the problem, but then mentions as the reason for her lateness that her children don't get ready on time. The latter should thus be the focus of the problem-solving process. As another example, a couple complains that they "are always arguing." Here, you might ask, "What do you argue about?" The topics of their arguments may then be the subject of problem-solving efforts.

Defining the problem may also mean breaking down a complex problem into its sub-components. For instance, if a couple's finances are in a tangle, this problem may have to be tackled one part at a time. One aspect might be helping the couple problem-solve around how to spend less each month. Although some goals are not easily defined in terms of their positive behaviors, as much as is possible, the focus should be on what people want, not what they don't want. For example, it could be "discuss finances calmly" rather than "not argue over money."

BRAINSTORMING

Brainstorming is the part of the problem-solving process in which the client is encouraged to come up with as many solutions as possible—even those that are silly, creative, outlandish, or impossible. If more than one person is taking part in the process, the social worker should ensure that feedback is obtained from everyone. One way to do this in a particularly unruly group or one in which there are dominating members is to ask each person in turn for an idea until several are posted. Sometimes it is only after people come up with a number of ideas that they become "warmed up" and consider other options. Some prompts for getting ideas generated include those listed in Table 7.4.

All solutions should be written down. Clients should be asked to avoid critical comments so that numerous options can be generated. Sometimes clients at this stage will attempt to dismiss certain ideas or argue about their feasibility. However, the social worker should redirect the brainstorming process, stating that the time for evaluating alternatives will come later. When people criticize, they should be asked to come up with a solution instead.

EVALUATING ALTERNATIVES

When evaluating alternatives, the patently irrelevant or impossible items are crossed out before each viable alternative is examined for its advantages and disadvantages. Sometimes in this process, clients will find that they need to collect more information. For example,

TABLE 7.4: **Brainstorming Prompts**

"What would _____ [an important person in a family member's life] say you might do about this?"

"What would _____ [people family members admire] do in this situation?"

Think about what you have done to solve other problems like this in the past.

Ask questions that prompt different classes of solutions (Foster & Robin, 1989):

"Are there consequences that might help Jody do her chores?"

"Are there some things that might motivate her to do her chores?"

"What are ways to change your routine that might help you?"

Make an off-the-wall or "crazy" suggestion yourself.

the couple with financial problems might need to find out more information about credit consolidation programs or credit counseling options.

CHOOSING AND IMPLEMENTING AN ALTERNATIVE

The next part of the problem-solving process is choosing and implementing an alternative. Here the social worker has the client select one or more strategies that seem to maximize benefits over costs. The social worker needs to consider any barriers that may arise and make sure there is a plan in place to overcome them. Role-playing may be necessary for any solution that has an interactional component. Finally, a client's commitment to following through with the plan should be assessed: "On a scale of 1 to 10, where 10 is that you are definitely going to do this, where are you?"

EVALUATING THE IMPLEMENTED OPTION

Evaluating the implemented option involves exploring with the client how the plan was enacted and its subsequent effect. Praise is used liberally for the elements of the plan that went well, as well as those parts that still need work. Lack of compliance should be a topic for discussion (see Chapter 9). If needed, the plan is then revised or a new option is selected from the list.

USING PROBLEM-SOLVING TRAINING WITH FAMILIES

The problem-solving process is not only taught to people on an individual basis, it is also a skill taught to couples and families. Some additional challenges are typically presented when problem-solving is presented in a family context (Foster & Robin, 2006). These are outlined along with some possible solutions in Table 7.5. Exercise 7.2 provides practice finding appropriate problems with which to use problem-solving and Exercise 7.3 allows you to try out this process using a client of your own.

COMMUNICATION SKILLS TRAINING

Communication skills cover a wide spectrum of interventions that include social skills, assertiveness, and negotiation skills. There are many advantages to improving communication. First, positive communication builds relationships and closeness with others, which in turn enhances social support (Clarke, Lewinsohn, & Hops, 1999). Second, such social support not only provides not only a source of positive reinforcement but also buffers individuals from stressful life events. In addition, processing the effects of problems with other

TABLE 7.5: Challenges to the Problem-Solving Process in Families

Problem	Possible Response
Family members may believe that the problem-solving process seems "fake."	Many new skills seem artificial at first. After the family becomes more adept at the skill, they can adapt it to suit its members.
Sometimes people complain that by focusing on a specific problem, the "real problem" is being ignored.	Problems manifest themselves in specific ways; they can be solved by coming up with a lot of ideas first and then picking an idea and working on it.
	Large, complex problems should be broken down into their constituent parts and worked at one at a time.
Certain family members exert more power than others and try to dominate the process.	Reassure the family that all members have the right to be heard and understood. Sometimes different definitions of the problem are necessary so that the problem is illuminated more fully.
For resistant, sullen, or passive members, ask them to assume roles that involve participation in the process, such as writing down solutions and reading them back, or writing down the pros and cons of viable alternatives.	Ask everyone in the room to give ideas.
	Openly discuss the consequences for those who go against the prevailing norms of the system.
	If parties come to an impasse on a certain solution—one side wants one idea implemented and the other side wants another—ask the couple or family to implement one solution one week (usually the children's), and if it doesn't work, try the next idea the following week.

EXERCISE 7.2: APPROPRIATE USE OF PROBLEM-SOLVING

Instructions: Given the following client scenario, what is a problem mentioned here that is appropriate for problem-solving? Explain your rationale.

Nikki, an 18-year-old white female, came to the university counseling center at the behest of her dormitory floor's residential adviser, who was concerned about Nikki's weight loss. Nikki admitted that she was "not happy" about coming to the center, but she liked the residential adviser and didn't want to "alienate" her. When she came to her initial session, Nikki appeared visibly emaciated and was wearing a long, oversized sweater and baggy sweatpants. At the beginning of the interview, she was guarded and answered questions with only a few words. But when she realized that the social worker "was not going to tell me I needed to gain weight like everyone else," she began to open up, although she spoke in a flat, matter-of-fact tone, even about painful subjects.

Nikki said she had begun to lose weight the summer of her senior year of high school, though her concerns about her weight had begun at age 13. Before that time she had been a "skinny kid," and that's how she wanted to stay. She admitted that

(continued)

she didn't want to grow up and thought that staying thin was a way to achieve this. She said she admired little girls' bodies (even girls as young as three and four), and thought they looked great.

During that summer, Nikki said that she was bored because there were no jobs for high school students in the midsized city where she lived. Losing weight gave her "something to do." Every day, she ate only two meals and jumped rope for 30 minutes. If she didn't exercise daily, she felt "fat" and "disgusted" with herself. Nikki said that before the summer, she didn't have the discipline to cut back on her food intake. At the same time, she said she had exercised and weighed herself almost every day since she was 14 years old. At five feet, four inches, she has never weighed more than 105 pounds.

_____

_____

_____

_____

EXERCISE 7.3: PROBLEM-SOLVING TRAINING

Consider a problem with which a client is struggling. It could be financial, a transportation issue, or how to handle a situation at work or with the family. Or do you have a family system with conflict? What issues could be used as the basis for problem-solving training with your clients?

_____

_____

_____

_____

_____

_____

TABLE 7.6: Using "I" Messages

Guideline	Example
"I" messages are those in which a person talks about his or her own position and feelings in a situation, rather than making accusatory comments about another person. The basic format for giving "I" messages is: I feel (the reaction) to what happened (a specific activating event).	"I feel worried when you stay out past curfew on Saturday night." The statement "How dare you stay out so late!" may make the other person feel defensive.
A good guideline for when to initiate the use of "I" messages is when people are interested in working on a relationship, or when they need someone to change his or her behavior because interaction with that person can't be avoided.	If a person can be easily avoided, then it might not be worth doing the work and taking the risk involved in making "I" messages.

people may change one's perspective on problem-generating Jevents. When a person can openly state feelings and reactions to interpersonal situations, other people understand clearly how they might continue their positive behaviors or change their negative behavior. This rationale of the importance of communication skills should be provided to clients so they become motivated to learn them.

The components of communication skills training include using "I" messages (see Table 7.6), reflective and empathic listening, making clear behavior change requests, and complimenting.

The purpose of reflective listening is to ensure that one understands the speaker's perspective. It decreases the tendency of people to draw premature conclusions about the intentions and meaning of another's statement. Reflective listening involves paraphrasing back the feelings and content of the speaker's message, with the format shown in Table 7.7.

A third component of communication skills training involves teaching people to make clear behavior requests of others. Such requests should have the qualities listed in Table 7.8.

Praising or complimenting is also considered an essential communication skill, as it reinforces desired behaviors in others so that the behaviors will continue to occur. (See Chapter 2 for guidelines.) Another purpose is to create a positive atmosphere in the relationship so that other interventions will be more effective when they are applied.

While communication skills seem fairly straightforward when they are laid out in this way, people typically have enormous difficulty learning these skills. Table 7.9 covers some of the common challenges, along with ways you as the social worker can respond.

TABLE 7.7: Reflective Listening

"What I hear you saying is..."
"You seem to feel...."
"You're feeling..."

Clear Behavior Requests

Request	Example
Specific vs. global	"Pick up your toys." vs. "Clean up around here."
Measurable	"I would like you to call once per day."
Stated as the presence of positive behaviors rather than the absence of negative behaviors	"Give me a chance to change my clothes and look over the mail when I come home, and then we can talk." rather than "Stop bothering me with your questions."

TABLE 7.9: **Challenges in Learning Communication Skills**

Challenges	Possible Solutions
People use "I" messages that are really disguised "you" messages (i.e., "I feel like you never listen to me.")	Remind people to talk about their feelings first (e.g., "I feel sad when….")
People make global statements about the other person rather than describing specific behaviors (e.g., "You never listen to me.")	Remind people to describe specific behaviors (e.g., "I tell you about my day, and you keep watching TV.")
People are hesitant to do reflective listening because they think that by reflecting another's feelings they are agreeing with the other person's version of events.	Reassure people that they don't have to agree with what the other person is saying; they just have to reflect back the content of the message (i.e., "You're saying that you feel sad when you tell me about your day and I'm watching TV."). Tell them that they will have a chance to state their side of the situation as well.
People ask for change from the other person that is stated in global terms (e.g., "if you could just be nice to me").	Indicate that change requests should be made as specific behaviors (e.g., "I would like you to turn off the TV when I'm telling you about my day.")
People say that they shouldn't have to ask for what they want—the other person should already know.	Remind people that others are not "mind-readers" and that we all find different things important, so the other person must be told what we consider important.
People are reluctant to praise others for the behaviors they want ("He should already be doing these things. He never says anything nice to me, so why should I say anything nice to him?"	Let people know that praise is important because it lets others know they are on track in giving us what we would like. Praise is also a reciprocal process, and positive feelings engendered by praise may lead to the other person praising in turn.

Example 7.3 shows some of the challenges inherent in learning new communications for a group of men who were court-ordered domestic violence offenders.

SOCIAL SKILLS TRAINING

Not every client will need this most fundamental level of communication: being able to exhibit the social skills that are successful at eliciting positive reinforcement from the

EXAMPLE 7.3: CHALLENGES IN LEARNING ABOUT COMMUNICATION SKILLS

Case #1: *This group involves men who have been mandated to treatment for domestic violence.*

Facilitator: Last week we started talking about communication skills, including the use of "I" statements. Let's hear from someone who has tried this out over the last week.

Jim: Yeah, I tried it but can't say it went any better than usual, which is to say pretty bad.

Facilitator: Could you tell us what happened?

Jim: Sure. I told my wife I resent always being the one to have to wash the car just because she never does. Then she goes ballistic, said she didn't care anything about the car—and things went downhill from there. So much for "I" statements.

Facilitator (turning to the rest of the group)**:** What do you think? How might Jim have worded this differently and possibly gotten a more positive reaction from his wife?

Carlos: Man, that's not the way you talk to your woman. We learned that. For starters, she probably got all riled up because you said she never washes the car. That's an attack, man, and she didn't like it.

Jim: So how would you have said it?

Carlos: Telling her how you feel was a good start. How about something like, "I feel resentful because it seems like I'm always the one washing the car." I gather from what she said that washing the car isn't high on her list of priorities. That's fair to say, right?

Jim: Yeah, I'm sure it isn't nowhere on her list of priorities.

Carlos: Then, how about if you say that and be happy if she helps out a little? What if you say, "I know a clean car is more important to me than to you, but how about if out of three months, you wash it one month, and I wash it two. I'd really appreciate that. It would mean a lot to me." What do you think of that?

Jim: Yeah, that might have gone down better.

Facilitator: Carlos, you made some good suggestions, and they included the main points we talked about last week. Who can tell us what particular communication skills Carlos used in rephrasing this request?

Dan: He didn't accuse his wife of doing anything wrong.

Facilitator: Yes, that's very important. What else?

Jim: The request is put into specific and measurable terms. I'd ask her to wash the car—that's specific—and every third month—that's measurable.

Facilitator: You got it! And the final thing we talked about. (Pause) Anyone? Okay, Jim's request is for a positive behavior. He's asking his wife to do something positive, not to stop doing something negative.

environment. Such skills lead to more positive interactions and help build or improve relationships. The most basic skills involve making eye contact, smiling at least once or more when in conversation with another person, saying something positive about the other person, and revealing some personal information (e.g., "I usually take the earlier bus.") When teaching social skills, the social worker should model these behaviors and then allow the client to rehearse.

The next skill that is addressed is when to start a conversation and what to say. Clients should be instructed that good times to start conversations are when the other person makes eye contact, when the other person says "hello," and when in a common situation (e.g., waiting for the bus, waiting in line). They should also be taught to avoid starting conversations when another person looks busy, preoccupied, or angry. Examples of conversational topics are recommended: weather, sports, and so on—anything that the individual might share in common with the other person. Finally, clients are given instruction in how to leave a conversation. In a large group, they can just say, "Excuse me," and leave with a smile. Suggestions for leaving a conversation in smaller groups of two to three people are "I think I'll go get something to eat" or "I'd like to talk to [so-and-so] over there, I'll see you later."

Example 7.4 illustrates training a client in use of social skills.

EXAMPLE 7.4: SOCIAL SKILLS TRAINING

Evelyn was a 19-year-old Hispanic female who had come to the Unites States from El Salvador a year ago. Evelyn's parents came to this country two years ago and at that time Evelyn and her sister had stayed behind with their grandmother. The reasons for referral to the school social work intern were that, according to teachers, Evelyn had difficulties making new friends, had poor school performance, and had low self-esteem. When she met with the intern, they conversed in Spanish, as the intern was also an immigrant from a Latin American country. Evelyn was frequently tearful and reported that it was hard for her to make new friends; she thought that she had nothing interesting to say to her classmates. That was why she spent most of the time by herself.

The social work intern decided to focus on helping Evelyn with her social skills. They started in the first session with some basic skills—making eye contact with other classmates, smiling at least once when in conversation, complimenting the other person ("I like your top."), and revealing some personal information ("I'm having a hard time with chemistry, too.") Evelyn named some specific instances in which she could practice these new skills (at the lunch table, while sitting and

(continued)

waiting for classes to start, while waiting for the bus to pick her up in the afternoon). They then rehearsed a couple of possible examples.

The intern met with Evelyn the following week, and Evelyn reported that she had been able to practice at least one social skill per day, as they had agreed. She realized that by making friendly overtures, other people typically responded in kind.

The work proceeded to making conversation. Since Evelyn enjoyed watching TV and listening to music, she noted that these could be topics of conversations with others ("Did you see _____ last night? What's your favorite show? Who do you like to listen to?") She also could talk about a situation that she had in common with another person. For example, since her bus was often late in the afternoon, she could talk to the other students at the bus stop about this topic. Again, the intern rehearsed the skills with Evelyn, who indicated specific possible people with whom she was interested in beginning conversations. Evelyn enjoyed the role-plays and was smiling when she left the next session.

The next time they met, Evelyn said that she'd been nervous but had followed through with the assignment of initiating at least one new conversation per day. She also reported that she now had lunch with classmates, and that she felt particularly attracted to three other students who seemed to be returning an interest in friendship. While the social work intern kept monitoring Evelyn's socializing, after this point they moved onto another goal of their work.

CONCLUSION

The topic of this chapter has been assisting clients with building new skills in order to elicit reinforcement from the environment and to help them manage life stressors and meet goals. Specifically, relaxation and mindfulness, problem-solving, communication skills, and social skills were discussed. Understand that each of these can also be delivered as a stand-alone intervention, even though they are usually employed within a package of other CBT techniques. To help you decide when you would use behavioral skill training, the next chapter will involve the development of treatment plans to meet individualized client needs and circumstances.

CHAPTER 8

DEVELOPING COPING PLANS

T his book has emphasized that readers should consult treatment manuals to benefit from experts' development of materials. However, it is not always possible to find a manual that fits the problem and the person you are seeing. As discussed in Chapter 5, it is possible to make adaptations in these cases. Another option and one that involves a more individualized approach is to come up with a plan based on the biopsychosocial assessment, covered in Chapter 2.

COPING PLANS

The construction of coping plans are demonstrated in Example 8.1 and Example 8.2. Example 8.3 involves the case from chapter 2 that was used to show behavioral chains, a detailing of the events and client reactions that led up to an unsafe behavior. I return to the example here to indicate how the social worker collaborates with the client to develop coping techniques so that the client's stress doesn't culminate in an incident of cutting.

Sometimes students find it hard to know what problems around which to design coping plans. The behavior should be one that the client has struggled against for some time, is under the client's individual control, and one that the client is motivated to take action on. (See Chapter 9 for more on helping a client build the motivation to change.) Exercise 8.1 gets you to look at which problems might involve an appropriate focus for coping plans. Exercise 8.2 is a blank template so that you can fill in a coping plan for a client problem.[1]

---

1. Behaviorists often refer to the ABC model of assessment, the acronym standing for antecedent, behavior, and consequences. However, and as mentioned in chapter 2, I simplify the model here. Through assessment, it's generally revealed that people employ a certain similar set of problem behaviors over time. Therefore, it is not seen as necessary to detail each time the behavior occurs but rather to consider the behavior a general set of responses. I also heavily rely on building client awareness of triggers for the behavior and then learning some tangible ways to counteract the cues for the behavior, the focus of designing coping plans.

EXAMPLE 8.1: BIOPSYCHOSOCIAL BEHAVIORAL ASSESSMENT AND COPING PLAN: CHILD PROTECTIVE SERVICES

Jennifer and her family currently have an ongoing case with Child Protective Services (CPS). Jennifer neglected her children because of her addiction to alcohol and crack/cocaine.

Biopsychosocial Domain	Antecedents (Triggers, Cues)	Antecedent Examples	Coping Plan
Biological	What uncomfortable physical states precede the occurrence of the problem?	Craving, restlessness, agitation	*Relaxation-training, breathing exercises, and other self-care activities.* *Distraction.* Use problem-solving to come up with a list of activities that can distract Jennifer from her physical tension and cravings. *Other coping with craving techniques.* Recall the negative consequences of use, employ self-talk strategies ("These feelings will pass, I've put too much effort into this, I don't want to give up now and have to start over again.")
Psychological	**Emotional—** What feeling states precede the occurrence of the problem?	Drug use to relieve feelings of depression about the state of her life—rift with her mother and sisters, neglect of children, involvement in CPS system	*Self-talk.* "These feelings don't last long—they never do. This will pass soon." *Cognitive restructuring.* Jennifer can learn how to target the negative beliefs that underlie her depression and substitute more positive and realistic thoughts. *Communication skills.* Communication skills can help Jennifer talk to people about her feelings and to request a behavior change when their actions are bringing her down. *Problem-solving.* Jennifer can use problem-solving to find different strategies to manage a depressed mood.
	Cognitive— What thoughts run through her mind, or what beliefs does she have about the problem?	"The only thing that will make me feel better is to use drugs."	*Cognitive restructuring.* This involves recognizing these automatic thoughts, challenging them, and replacing them with more positive thoughts.

(continued)

Biopsychosocial Domain	Antecedents (Triggers, Cues)	Antecedent Examples	Coping Plan
Social	Day-to-day cues, problematic social interactions that cue the problem	She lives in a crime-infested, low-income, urban community and often sees people she knows who use drugs.	*Avoidance.* Jennifer can be taught how to avoid friends with whom she parties (i.e., not calling them or stopping by, not calling back when they call, and staying inside when they might be out on the streets).
		Conflict with others, such as neighbors, her mother, and men in her life cue her to use drugs.	*Self-talk.* "My children come first. I can do this. I am making the right choice."
			Communication skills. Jennifer can learn how to resist the offers of friends to use alcohol and drugs. Also, these skills can be used to resolve conflict with others instead of using drugs.
			Social skills. Jennifer can learn how to use skills to meet people who don't use substances.
			Problem-solving. Jennifer can use the problem-solving process to determine her options for raising income or tapping into other resources so she can live in a different neighborhood.

EXAMPLE 8.2: BIOPSYCHOSOCIAL BEHAVIORAL ASSESSMENT AND COPING PLAN: SKIN PICKING

Ellie, a white female in her mid-20s, has sought the help of a social worker for her 10-year habit of picking her skin, which occurs on average about an hour a day.

Biopsychosocial Domain	Antecedents (Triggers, Cues)	Antecedent Examples	Coping Plan
Biological	What uncomfortable physical states precede the problem occurrence?	Tired (at nighttime) When getting ready for bed and washing her face, she starts to attend to skin blemishes and then is triggered to start picking at them.	*Problem-solve.* Figure out activities that she might find at least slightly relaxing to ease the transition into sleep, particularly those that are physical in nature, such as taking a hot shower, applying body lotion, or using a heating pads. *Avoidance.* Avoid having the lights off so she can avoid seeing the skin cue. *Prayer.* Use this ritual at bedtime instead of the ritual of skin picking.
Psychological	Emotional— What feeling states precede the occurrence of the problem?	Avoids feelings Obsessive thinking Unsure of what to do with her future	*Acknowledging feelings.* Record feelings and allow their experience. *Behavior activation.* Avoid rumination and try out different volunteer organizations, hobbies, and activities and schedule these and other pleasurable activities. *Problem-solving.* What new activities could she get involved with? *Problem-solving.* What pleasurable activities could she try that would help her relax and enjoy herself more?
	Cognitive— What thoughts run through her mind, or what beliefs does she have about the problem?	"What's the use?"	*Cognitive restructuring.* Challenge the thoughts of "What's the use of doing anything to feel better?"
Social	Day-to-day cues, problematic social interactions that cue the problem	New to a large urban area that is expensive to live in Holds a job that she finds unsatisfying	*Problem-solving and behavior activation around new activities.* Keep attending her church, which has a lot of young, single congregants, and join in activities sponsored there.

EXAMPLE 8.3: COLLABORATIVE CONVERSATION WITH CLIENT TO COME UP WITH COPING TECHNIQUES

Social Worker: Now, let's see if you think there are any places where skills could be used to change the outcome.

Taryn: I really can't think of anything. All this stuff just seems to happen to me. I don't know that there is anything I can really do about it.

Social Worker: First, I think there are actually a couple of skills you already implemented and maybe we can start there.

Taryn: It didn't seem like I used any skills.

Social Worker: What about when you were waiting to see Chris at the jail?

Taryn: Well, I spent time texting with some of my friends. But that was when things were allright.

Social Worker: You still used your supports. I know it is easier to do this when things are going well, but we need to think about how you can do things like this even when things aren't going so well. When else do you think that skills might have been involved?

Taryn: Well, when I was talking to Chris, even though I was really angry and hurt, I didn't lose it. I kept it together and even tried to change the topic to make the visit better.

Social Worker: Exactly!

Taryn: But, I told you how well that went—he just kept throwing it in my face.

Social Worker: Yes, unfortunately, sometimes even when we use skills well, our environment doesn't change the way we hope it would. However, if a skill doesn't work, we can always consider trying another one. Let's see where else you think skills might be helpful in the behavioral analysis we worked on.

Taryn: I know that I tend to get really down when I'm alone. It probably wasn't the best idea to go home after my visit with Chris. I just kept thinking about what had happened earlier. My cousin Chaundra is pretty good to talk to. I could have tried to go over to her house. She is usually home during the day.

Social Worker: That sounds like a great start. What other skills might be helpful?

Taryn: We've been talking a lot about changing emotions. I know I was feeling really upset and hurt. Maybe I could do something to try to change those emotions.

Social Worker: That's an excellent idea—do you have anything specific in mind?

Taryn: There is a park by my house. I have been trying to go there a couple times a week. It kinda helps me feel calm. I like to watch the kids playing there.

Social Worker: You're doing really well with this. Are there any other things you can think of?

Taryn: No, nothing else really comes to mind.

Social Worker: I have one other thought. You did mention that after you cut, you thought about your mom and your daughter. I wonder if we couldn't use thoughts of them a little earlier to help you change?

(continued)

Taryn: Yeah, that sounds like it might work, but how would I use it?

Social Worker: Well, I know that your mom and your daughter mean a lot to you. If you were thinking of them, do you think you would cut?

Taryn: Well, it would be a lot harder. I really do want to be a good mom and a good daughter.

Social Worker: This probably won't be easy, though. I know that your thoughts were pretty upsetting that day. Is there any way we could get you to think of your mom or your daughter, even if you were feeling really upset?

Taryn: I do carry a picture of my daughter with me. She does make me smile.

Social Worker: What is your favorite memory of you and your daughter?

Taryn: We went to the beach last year. She just kept on laughing and splashing in the water. I think that is my favorite memory.

Social Worker: Let's use that memory and your picture of your daughter. Over the next week I want you to practice thinking about being at the beach that day and using your picture when you start to feel down. If we start doing this when you are just a little upset, we can get you in the habit of using this skill. When this happens, our chances of you using it when you are even more upset are even better. This might need some practice, though.

Taryn: Yeah. It is hard for me to calm down, but if I practice this I think it could work.

Social Worker: Great! Let's give it a shot.

EXERCISE 8.1: COPING PLAN TARGETS

Exercise Instructions: Given the information provided about which problems may be appropriate for coping plans, circle the following examples that would NOT work as a target for a coping plan.

1. Substance use disorder
2. Physical abuse
3. Teenage pregnancy
4. Cutting
5. Anger
6. Poverty
7. Neighborhood crime
8. Depression
9. Anxiety
10. Homelessness

EXERCISE 8.2: COPING PLAN TEMPLATE

Instructions: Complete this chart with a client who struggles with a problem behavior.

Biopsychosocial Domain	Antecedents (Triggers, Cues)	Antecedents Examples	Coping Plan
Biological	What uncomfortable physical states precede the problem occurrence?		
Psychological	**Emotional**—What feeling states precede the occurrence of the problem?		
	Cognitive—What thoughts run through her mind, or what beliefs does she have about the problem?		
Social	Day-to-day cues, problematic social interactions that cue the problem		

CONCLUSION

This chapter ties in with material presented in Chapter 2, which centered on the assessment process of figuring out the cues and behavioral chains leading up to a problem behavior. The completed biopsychosocial spiritual assessment leads logically and naturally to goal-setting and intervention. This represents a more individualized approach, aside from the use of existing treatment manuals, and its preparation with the client can help the client develop ways to cope with and change triggers.

SECTION FIVE

COLLABORATION

MOTIVATION TO CHANGE AND CBT

When considering the use of CBT for client problems, the first part of working collaboratively with clients is to determine whether they are ready for the action-oriented steps involved. This chapter discusses the transtheoretical stages of change model and the place of CBT within a client's readiness to change. Motivational interviewing is also introduced as a way to help client motivation to change and to use CBT.

THE TRANSTHEORETICAL CHANGE MODEL AND CBT

Developed by Prochaska and colleagues (Connors, Donovan, & DiClemente, 2001; Prochaska & Norcross, 1984, 1994), the transtheoretical stages of change model offers a conceptualization of changing problem behaviors that follows a stage model (as the name suggests) that is defined in terms of motivation. The basic idea is that a variety of theoretical orientations may be able to help clients, but that certain techniques will be more useful when the client's motivation level matches them. The model offers the practitioner a way to systematize theoretical choices. Six stages of change have been formulated. They will be described here, along with how CBT integrates into the stages.

PRECONTEMPLATION

In precontemplation, the individual believes there is no problem behavior and thus is unwilling to do anything about it. At this stage, the individual sees the problem behavior as possessing more advantages than disadvantages. Typically, individuals in this stage are defensive and resistant about their behavior. They lack awareness of the problem. They do not come voluntarily to services and are usually coerced or pressured to do so by others. Therefore, they are often unwilling to actively participate with intervention.

At this stage, CBT techniques are not the focus. In the precontemplation stage, the practitioner, rather than targeting behavioral change in the client, should focus instead on building the client's motivation. William Miller and Stephen Rollnick are the developers of motivational interviewing (Miller & Rollnick, 2012). A collaborative approach to change, motivational interviewing allows for exploration of the problem—the needs it serves for the client and the negative consequences to the individual in terms of biological and psychological harm or, just as likely, social relationships that the client values. The practitioner empathetically listens, avoiding direct advice or pressuring the client. In order to move to the next stage, clients themselves need to reach the point of deciding that the disadvantages of the behavior may outweigh perceived advantages.

The only time CBT may be of use in the precontemplation stage is for a relative of a client with a drinking or drug problem. This relative must also be bothered by the problem and is likely more motivated for change to happen than the actual client. In the area of substance use disorder, several models of behavioral treatment were developed simultaneously—reinforcement training (Sisson & Azrin, 1986), unilateral therapy (Thomas & Ager, 1993), and the pressures to change model (Barber & Gilbertson, 1997). The common focus of these models is operant conditioning, the subject of Chapter 3. Relatives—usually the partners—are taught how to support the person for cutting down on drinking and for seeking treatment. They are also taught how to ignore drinking behavior and allow the person to suffer his or her own consequences for the problem.

CONTEMPLATION

In the contemplation stage, individuals begin to consider if perhaps a problem does exist. They are engaged in a process of evaluating the advantages and disadvantages of the problem. They also may go on to examine the feasibility and costs of changing the behavior. Here, they may feel distress in their conflict about the problem. During this stage, individuals are not yet prepared to take action; instead, change may be ahead, in the next six months.

The practitioner continues on the path of motivational interviewing, with more emphasis on boosting the value of change. CBT may come in at this point in terms of self-monitoring and finding alternative reinforcers. Through *self-monitoring*, individuals gain awareness of the frequency and intensity of the behavior, the cues that elicit it, and the consequences that follow. *Alternative reinforcers* are found that take the place of the problem behavior for meeting the person's needs. For example, a person may be referred to Alcoholics Anonymous to find a social network that is supportive of abstinence to replace a pro–substance use group of friends. Identifying social support systems is critical during this stage, so that others can promote change efforts.

DETERMINATION

In determination (also called preparation), the individual is poised to change in the next month or so. At this point, clients are ready to set goals and develop a change plan.

Here the client might be more interested in developing skills to resist and cope with the problem behavior. Such cognitive-behavioral skills may involve learning and rehearsing of relaxation training, visualization of successful outcomes, cognitive restructuring, communication skills, and avoidance of environmental cues, before the client goes into high-risk situations.

ACTION

In the action stage, the individual begins to modify the problem behavior and/or the environment, in an effort to follow suggested strategies and activities for change. The practitioner should acknowledge the difficulties associated with the early stages of change and empathize with the client. Continued appraisal of high-risk situations and coping strategies to overcome these are a mainstay at this point. Alternative reinforcers to problem behaviors should also be applied. Assessment of social support systems continues to be essential, so that others are a helpful resource for change rather than a hindrance. This stage may have an almost exclusive focus on cognitive-behavioral strategies, such as using learned coping skills and cognitive restructuring.

MAINTENANCE

In the maintenance stage, sustained change has occurred for at least six months. Avoiding slips or relapses is the focus of the work, most of which involves cognitive-behavioral interventions at this point (Prochaska & Norcross, 1994). The social worker continues to help the individual find alternative sources of satisfaction and enjoyment and to promote any lifestyle changes. Additionally, the social worker assists in clients' practice with coping skills and their application, guiding awareness of any cognitive distortions that might lead back to slips (e.g., "Life is no fun without drinking.").

RELAPSE

Although not seeing relapse as inevitable, DiClimente, Prochaska and associates put relapse into a strengths-based perspective that considers change not as a linear process but one that proceeds in an upward spiraling way. Each time people advance through the change process, they gain greater insight into high-risk situations and learn more strategies to avoid or manage them. The social worker at this point can help build motivation to initiate the change effort once more. The decisional balance technique from motivational interviewing will be the topic of the next section. Table 9.1 summarizes the stages of change and their relationship to CBT. In Exercise 9.1, you will have a chance to think about the place in the change process of your current clients and the accompanying relevance of CBT techniques.

TABLE 9.1: Transtheoretical Stages of Change Model and Where CBT Techniques Fit

Stage	Description	What CBT Techniques Are Involved?
Precontemplation	Coerced or mandated Client doesn't think there is a problem Client doesn't want to do anything to change the problem	None. Build collaborative stance with the client; allow exploration of the problem— its advantages and disadvantages. Reinforce change statements
Contemplation	Client is weighing the advantages and disadvantages of change.	Self-monitoring is used so the client can learn more about the advantages (what is reinforcing about the problem) and disadvantages of the problem (what is negative about it in terms of biological, psychological, and social issues?)
Determination (preparation)	Client is getting ready to change and putting a plan into place.	Client learns how to find and use alternate reinforcers; develops a variety of individualized coping skills to manage without the problem; learns avoidance techniques; learns how to change environmental cues and contingencies
Action	Client is making the change	Implement strategies developed; test the plan
Relapse	Client may go back to the problem behaviour	Prevent against high-risk situations; learn from and develop new strategies for slips

---

EXERCISE 9.1: TRANSTHEORETICAL STAGES OF CHANGE

Exercise Instructions: Consider the clients with whom you currently work. Assign them de-identified names or just use the numbers already in place. Write in the person's current stage of change and what tells you that. In the third column, list the strategies you have been using. In the fourth column, write what is advised according to the transtheoretical change model. Is this different from or the same as what you had already been doing with the client?

Client	Stage of Change	Strategies	Transtheoretical Model
1.			
2.			
3.			

The decisional balance was designed as a motivational interviewing tool, to help persons process through ambivalence about whether they have a problem and whether they should change. The strengths-based assumption is that people demonstrate ambivalence about rather than resistance to change. The practitioner allows for nonjudgmental exploration, avoiding labeling and arguing for change. Viewed from a CBT perspective, the decisional balance assessment can be used to collect valuable information about what is reinforcing about the problem. The decisional assessment also looks at disadvantages (including punishers) of the behavior (e.g., feeling hung over, cravings for more of the substance, missing work, making others disappointed and angry).

Following is a description of the steps to take in using the decisional balance (Miller & Rollnick, 2012).

1. ASSESS ADVANTAGES OF THE PROBLEM BEHAVIOR

When clients first begin to work on a problem behavior they may feel defensive about the behavior and worry that the practitioner is going to tell them what to do. Beginning the process by examining the advantages of the problem behavior is helpful because it is less threatening. Asking clients what they like about their behavior or "what they get out of it" disarms their defensiveness. People enjoy having their perspective heard and, consequently, feel less judged by the practitioner.

They are also given credit for the fact that the problem behavior, though seemingly irrational and perhaps even destructive, is subject to the principles of operant conditioning, and exists because it is being reinforced by an event that comes after it. Operant conditioning is discussed in Chapter 3 so will only briefly be touched on here. For example, a person may report that she uses alcohol to feel better when she is depressed. Another person may say that drinking eases the strain of talking to others. Letting people know that their behavior is being reinforced may help them understand the behavior more, and may provide a rationale for the use of CBT interventions. Just as a behavior is learned from the reinforcing contingencies, so too can it be unlearned, with more positive behaviors to take its place.

Some readers may wonder whether asking about the good things about a behavior will condone it. The answer is "no." Asking what a client gets out of a behavior facilitates the practitioner's and the client's understanding of the problem and the advantages associated with the behavior. As a social worker, you are not saying that you think it is a good idea that the client continue with a problem behavior, just that you understand the client's perspective. As part of the exploration, you can ask clients if they would be interested in trying to meet these needs in alternative ways, even if they are currently uninterested in reducing or ameliorating the behavior. As a common example, people report that drinking eases the strain of talking to others. In such cases, they may be willing to explore how they can manage social situations in different ways that don't involve alcohol.

2. ASSESS DISADVANTAGES OF THE PROBLEM BEHAVIOR

In the process of talking about what clients like about their problem behavior, they will sometimes spontaneously initiate discussion of its downsides. If not, you can say, "Now that we've talked about what you get out of [the drug use, not taking your medication, staying in this relationship, not complying with the program], let's talk about the not so good things." When people turn to the disadvantages of their behavior, they should be encouraged to speak about these at some length, giving concrete examples. For instance, you could say, "You've said you don't like the way you act when you've been drinking a lot. Can you give me a recent example of when this happened?" By describing in detail specific incidences, people begin to hear that the problem behavior has landed them in services, and the process of beginning to talk themselves into change can begin.

Here you can also ask clients about their values and goals for their lives, such as their children, their other relationships, and their professional aspirations.

- "What sorts of things are important to you?"
- "Once the addiction or relationship is behind you, what do you see as your ideal situation?"
- "What steps can you take now to get closer to this?"

You can then work to develop cognitive discrepancy in the client by posing statements contrasting the values and goals that have been named with the problem behavior. For instance, for a woman who loses control of her anger but identifies that her children are the most important thing in her life you can say, "You didn't want your daughter to see you out of control like that. You want to be a good role model to your daughter, and her seeing you getting that mad and hitting her does not fit in with the idea for yourself as a parent." Use the format in Exercise 9.2 to determine both the advantages and disadvantages of a behavior in a decisional balance assessment.

3. ASSESS ADVANTAGES OF CHANGING

The first two steps just described work to help people decide whether the behavior is a problem. The second part of the decisional balance has to do with exploring whether a person wants to do something about the problem. To ask about the advantages of changing, you can make such statements as, "The fact that you're here indicates that at least a part of you thinks it's time to do something. What are the reasons you see for making a change? What are the good things about changing?" (Miller & Rollnick, 2012). In discussing the advantages of changing a behavior, you can again highlight the clients' values and goals for their lives, and how change may allow for the expression of these values and goals, as shown in Table 9.2.

Motivational interviewing is concerned with reinforcing client statements about change. This is also in line with CBT concepts of reinforcement. Therefore, be on the lookout for such client statements and reflect these, thus reinforcing them. Moyers et al. (2009) found that when a practitioner reflected client statements about change, people

EXERCISE 9.2: DECISIONAL BALANCE

For a client who is not yet ready to change a problem behavior, use a decisional balance assessment.

Make a list of all the advantages of the behavior:

Make a list of the disadvantages of the behavior:

What did the client conclude at the end of this exploration?

Are there any preliminary goals at this point (e.g., self-monitoring to continue to assess the role of drinking in a person's life)?

TABLE 9.2: Example Dialogue

Client: I'm sick of my children not talking to me.
Social Worker: You'd like to have a better relationship with your children, and they like to be with you when you're clean.

TABLE 9.3: Example Dialogue

Client: I want to change. I just don't know if I can.
Social Worker: You know changing is important.
Client: I really should leave him, but it's too overwhelming to think about.
Social Worker: You're pretty sure leaving him is the right decision.

were more likely to change their behavior (substance use disorder). Watch, therefore, for even veiled change statements, and reinforce the aspect of the message that is about changing, as shown in Table 9.3.

4. ASSESS DISADVANTAGES OF CHANGING

The final step in the decisional balance is to talk about the disadvantages of changing. Although it may feel that you are now allowing clients to talk themselves out of change, you should not ignore this side of the equation, as it may represent barriers that will get in the way of change if they are not addressed. Although your clients will have their individual reasons, based on their unique circumstances, experiences, and preferences, there are common reasons why people resist change (see Table 9.4). Included are certain belief systems that can be explored and reframed for clients. In the process you can explain how CBT works to address some of their concerns (Beck, 2005).

TABLE 9.4: Arguments Against Change and Reframes

Reasons to Stay the Same	Reframe
Too much effort The effort involved in changing, forging new habits, and making a new routine is too great.	• Doing nothing means that nothing will change either. • Structure (having things to do) is a good way to combat feelings of helplessness and powerlessness. • The approach is step-by-step, so that habits can be built up over time at a manageable level.
Fear of change	• Validate that change is scary; however, also ask, "How well is what you're doing now working?"
Fear of being weak	• It takes a lot of courage to admit and face a problem. • The skills learned with CBT can be learned and applied to a variety of life circumstances.
Discomfort It might feel uncomfortable or even painful to deal with these problems.	• Pain and discomfort are already associated with the problem and will continue if nothing else changes. • If a person changes, he or she will increase the chance of feeling better.

(continued)

Reasons to Stay the Same	Reframe
Reluctance "to dig up the past"	• The CBT approach is oriented toward the present and current functioning.
Fear of failure	• The risk of trying must be attempted before any success is possible.
Although change may be desirable, it's also scary because it's an unknown. The problem feels comfortable and familiar, in contrast.	• CBT involves small, concrete steps toward change. It is not an instantaneous, "all-or-nothing" prospect.
Identity loss	CBT is concerned with changing specific beliefs and behaviors rather than a personality overhaul. Change occurs with small steps, so it can be managed over time rather than all at once.
Some people will feel as if they are losing a significant part of themselves, their identity, if they make a change.	
Some people don't know how to go about changing.	CBT offers a structured, fairly directive approach.
Fear of losing people who are important to the client.	Validate the losses that will accompany change. Decide whether the losses are worth the potential gain (better health, developing healthier relationships, and meeting goals in life).
For example, people whose social life revolves around drinking may recognize they will have to leave a circle of friends to stay sober.	
Beliefs about helplessness (Beck, 2005): "I can't make changes." "I'm too helpless." "I have no control." "I can't do anything about it." "What will happen, will happen" and other fatalistic attitudes.	Engage in exploration, helping people assess the degree of control they have over a problem by asking them in which ways they have positive control over a problem and in which ways they have negative control. For instance, "Things I can do to convince my child welfare worker that I am ready to have my kids returned" vs. "Things I can do that will make my child welfare worker believe my children should be returned."
Letting others "off the hook"	In CBT, the goal isn't personality change, but rather learning new behaviors in order to cope with a problem that may have originated outside the person's control. What is under people's control is not change of another person but how to make themselves feel better and to meet other life goals.
Some people believe that if they change, they will be letting other people, who may have played a role in the problem developing, "off the hook." Common examples are parents who believe their misbehaving child should be the focus of intervention; adult children who blame their mother and father's parenting mistakes as contributing toward lifelong problems in a child; and ex-partners who have abandoned or hurt them. In these situations, clients may feel like victims of others, and that they shouldn't have to be the ones to exert change efforts. Indeed, they may even believe that if they do anything differently, it would shift the blame to the themselves for the problem.	

At the same time, we recognize that there are parts of clients' environment (housing, transportation, employment, income, and neighborhood safety, for example) that our clients are not in control of. The resultant feelings of frustration, fear, and helplessness need to be understood and validated. Additionally, the social worker must apply interventions at the appropriate system level so that some of the environmental hardships can be ameliorated. At the individual level, simultaneously, we can work to maximize client's self-efficacy, characterized by an internal sense of control and a belief that one can influence one's environment. Increased self-efficacy may lead to positive behavior change (Miller & Rollnick, 2012) and is an important resilience factor in coping with adverse life events (Wachs, 2000; Werner & Smith, 2001).

To pull all this information together, now use Exercise 9.3 to carry out the second part of the decisional balance: identifying the advantages and disadvantages of changing a behavior.

EXERCISE 9.3: ADVANTAGES AND DISADVANTAGES OF CHANGING

For a client who is not yet ready to change a problem behavior, complete the last two aspects of the decisional balance.

Make a list of all the advantages of changing the behavior:

1.
2.
3.
4.
5.

Make a list of all the disadvantages of changing the behavior:

1.
2.
3.
4.
5.

How did you address the disadvantages?

(continued)

How did you develop discrepancy?

What was the client's conclusion at the end of this exploration?

Are there any preliminary goals at this point? For example, a person who is still not sure whether she wants to quit drinking decides that one of her goals is to seek out activities that don't revolve around drinking. In this way, she may be able to get more environmental structure and supports in place before she stops entirely. Or, a person who is stuck in an abusive relationship might work on the belief system that she is helpless to change.

CONCLUSION

This chapter provides a framework for how CBT is positioned within the stages of change model. The variety of CBT techniques are discussed in terms of where they fall within the stages. Motivational interviewing was presented as a way to help people bolster their motivation to tackle their problems and to progress through the stages of change. Although motivational interviewing is much more than the decisional balance, this technique does provide a basis for PRODUCTIVE conversation about the possibility of change and the use of CBT.

TEST YOUR SKILLS EXERCISE 9.1: COLLABORATION SKILLS

1. A client has been mandated to see you because of a driving under the influence (DUI) charge. He initially seemed distraught about his legal involvement and said he was willing to do "whatever it took" and agreed to CBT. However, now he says, "I'm just not sure that my drinking is that bad, so doing all this stuff doesn't seem relevant."

What would be the first thing you would do?
   a. Remind him that he had received a DUI and that his alcohol problem seemed rather serious.
   b. Emphasize that it was important to follow through with the CBT as agreed.
   c. Make a reflecting statement, such as "You're not sure that your drinking is something to work on right now."
   d. Ask about the advantages and disadvantages of his alcohol use.

2. Referring again to the scenario above, what might be other ways to intervene following your initial response? Indicate the one that would NOT be appropriate.
   a. Explore what he gets out of his drinking.
   b. Renegotiate the goal of abstinence into CBT skill building so that he can meet some of his needs other than through alcohol.
   c. Confront him about his alcohol use, showing evidence of how people have been killed in DUI accidents.
   d. Reflect both sides of his ambivalence: "On the one hand, you feel like it's not worth examining your triggers, since you're not sure drinking is a problem, and on the other hand, you've been hearing a lot of complaints from your family and friends about your drinking, and that DUI charge was really a shock and cost you a lot."

3. "I don't know, do you really think this is such a big deal after all? Maybe we should just move on to something else. I'm not sure that I can change my thoughts and behaviors—I'm pretty set in my ways."

Such a statement may indicate there is a need to revisit motivation in which area?

   a. To take active steps to solve their problems.
   b. To be ready to confront the problem.
   c. To buy in to CBT as a model of change.
   d. All of the above.

CHAPTER 10

COLLABORATIVE DELIVERY OF PSYCHOEDUCATION

U p until now, the techniques themselves of CBT have been the focus of the chapters. We now turn to the methods by which CBT is delivered:

- Psychoeducation
- Modeling
- Behavior rehearsal
- Reinforcement
- Homework

A theme of this book is the need to deliver cognitive-behavioral interventions in a collaborative manner that is attuned to social work values and ethics. Even though CBT is an information-oriented and fairly directive approach, it must be applied in an individualized way and based on a solid relationship foundation between the social worker and the client. Until clients feel understood, they won't be ready to embark on the fairly active steps that CBT requires. This chapter begins with psychoeducation—the provision of education about the CBT model and its techniques in a way that allows for active engagement, exploration, and interaction with the information presented. Also discussed in this chapter is how to deliver information on CBT that is sensitive to the culture of the participants.

PROVIDING A RATIONALE FOR CBT

Once you have determined through your assessment that there is a problem that can be addressed through CBT, you will have to provide a rationale for why CBT may be the ideal approach (see Exercise 10.1). One way is to provide a connection between a person's problem and the approach: "You've talked about not being able to relate to people unless you're drinking. What we can do is work on what you can say to start conversations and keep them going and how to practice being around people sober." Another way is to mention the evidence basis: "For children with the kind of anger and defiance you've described, there are many studies that show this is the most effective way to intervene." For other ideas and rationales that have to do with involving parents in operant conditioning (parent training) for their children's discipline problems, see Table 10.1.

EDUCATION ON THE CBT MODEL

Once a rationale has been provided and client initial buy-in has been obtained, clients can be educated on how CBT is conceptualized. You can use a presentation similar to that in Figure 10.1, possibly modifying it, depending on the cognitive abilities of the client,

---

TABLE 10.1: Engaging Parents in Intervention

Guideline	Sample Response
Emphasize the dominant role that the parent plays in the child's role and downplay your own importance.	"You are the most important person to your child, more than I ever would be in my hour a week I see her. If I work with you, you can be much more effective than I could ever hope to be."
Explain children's cognitive limitations.	"Young children have a difficult time learning a new behavior in one setting, such as my office, and then generalizing that skill to another context. When you learn what I will be teaching him, you can prompt him for these behaviors at home and then reinforce him for doing them."
Explain the limitation of children's attention.	"Children (even ones who can listen and follow directions) will only be able to focus on one subject, especially if the subject is an uncomfortable one, for a short time."
Mention research showing that training parents to change behavior in their children is more effective for young children with conduct problems (up to age 12) than working with the children individually using CBT (McCart, Priester, Davies, & Azen, 2006).	"Some tentative evidence even suggests that working only with the parents is more effective than working with both the parents and the child" (Lundahl et al., 2006).
Consider the NASW Code of Ethics mandate: "Social workers understand that relationships between and among people are an important vehicle for change. Social workers engage people as partners in the helping process. Social workers seek to strengthen relationships among people in a purposeful effort to promote, restore, maintain, and enhance the wellbeing of individuals, families, social groups, organizations, and communities."	This ethic demands that we engage parents as partners in the helping process with the recognition that the relationship between parent and child is an important vehicle for change.

EXERCISE 10.1: CBT RATIONALE

Consider a client whose problems you believe are appropriate for CBT. Explain in a sample dialogue how you might offer such a rationale:

_____

_____

_____

following the steps outlined here. In Exercise 10.2, you will be asked to consider how you would do this with a particular client whose problem may be suited for CBT.

1. Share a visual of the feeling, thoughts, action triad (Figure 10.1) and how they relate to each other, giving primacy to how thoughts and behaviors are influential, to help people grasp the model.

2. Explain that the nature of change in cognitive-behavioral theory is apparent in its hyphenated term. That is, clients can be helped to change in three ways (Young, Rygh, Weinberger, & Beck, 2008):
   - Cognitively, by teaching them how to identify and change distorted thinking.
   - Behaviorally, by offering skills training to improve coping capability.
   - Affectively, by teaching people to recognize their feelings and triggers and to work on managing and changing uncomfortable and painful feelings through changing their thoughts, changing their actions, and learning coping skills.

The techniques from each of the three domains of thinking, behavior, and emotion are detailed in Table 10.2.

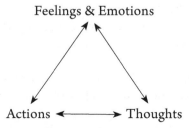

FIGURE 10.1: Visual Connection between Thoughts, Feelings, and Behaviors.

TABLE 10.2: Domains of Change in Cognitive-Behavioral Therapy

Domain	Cognitive-Behavioral Techniques
Actions	*Skill-building:*
	Social skills
	Problem-solving
	Communication
	Assertiveness
Thoughts	Stopping irrational thoughts
	Increasing positive self-talk
Feelings	Changing thoughts
	Changing actions
	Learning relaxation and other coping skills

EXERCISE 10.2: CBT APPLICATIONS

Consider a client whose problems you believe are appropriate for CBT. Explain how you will instruct the client on the CBT model and how it applies to his or her problems.

_____

_____

_____

GUIDELINES WHEN OFFERING INFORMATION AND TEACHING NEW SKILLS

The majority of this chapter focuses on how the social worker can deliver information on new behaviors and skills that the client can learn to ameliorate their problem. Guidelines are provided here for how this can be done in a process-based way, and in a way that promotes collaboration between the social worker and the client.

1. First, ensure that basic needs—food, clothing transportation, and housing—have been met, as these take obvious priority over learning CBT.

2. Explore clients' situations and their feelings before launching into the provision of information. A client who doesn't feel that she has explored with a practitioner fully the nature of her particular situation may feel misunderstood if the practitioner launches too quickly into teaching mode. Ask the client's permission for you to offer more information: "Would it be all right if we took a moment and explored a statement I notice you keep making about yourself?"

3. Avoid the use of technical explanations. As you may have noticed, CBT is full of its own terms, but using such technical information with clients might only alienate them. The words "learning" or "rewards," for instance, can be used instead of "reinforcement," "contingencies," and "stimulus conditions" to make information more understandable. What has the person already tried? Before giving out information, the social worker needs to know how the person has already tried to handle his or her difficulties. Asking about problem-solving attempts gives people credit for their efforts and a sense of their own competence. In this way, the social worker also acquires important information for intervention purposes. First, the social worker learns about what has been tried, and in what ways. "When you say you used time-out, tell me, what did you do? What happened?" The social worker may find that efforts were applied inconsistently or in a manner that sabotaged the client's success. Sometimes people may have to be educated about a more effective way to apply possible solutions. Second, if strategies have been applied correctly but have still not been helpful, the social worker may avoid the same tactics and try something else (Murphy, 2008). This process of asking questions about clients' previous problem-solving attempts contributes toward building a collaborative alliance around the best course of action that will take place.

4. Once you have offered information and have discussed it with the client, elicit the client's views on how he or she might use information you have provided.

Example: "Now that we've talked about how you can respond to your child's feelings about the sexual abuse, tell me what you will say when she brings it up."

---

5. Ask clients about their knowledge of a particular topic and how it applies to them.

Example: "What do you already know about Alzheimer's?" or "You've said you've tried timeout. Tell me what happened when you did that. Walk me through the steps."

---

6. Ask deductive questions so that clients can make their own connections and form their own conclusions.

> Example: If a parent says she gives in to her children when they whine, the social worker could ask, "What are the consequence of 'giving in'?" and "What do children learn when we give in to whining?" For a caregiver of an older adult parent with dementia, the social worker can inquire, "What happens when you don't ask for help?"

7. Pay attention to clients' verbal and nonverbal cues. These might include lack of eye contact, one-word responses, yawning, hostile stares, or a rigid posture with arms folded across the chest.

> Example: "I notice that you keep yawning, and I was wondering what your thoughts are on what we're talking about today."

8. Ask people to describe the skill in their own words.

> Example: "We've talked a lot about ways you can relax when you start having symptoms of anxiety. Just to make sure you're confident about what you can do, what will you do next time you feel your heart racing and you have difficulty swallowing?"

9. Elicit clients' reactions to the material.

> Example: "What do you think about these ideas?"

10. When people complain about techniques seeming artificial or "not like life really is," reassure them about the discomfort associated with change and trying out new behaviors until they become a habit. You can also inquire about any adaptations that can be made, so that using the technique can feel like it is more within their comfort zone. Ask for ideas on what might be helpful instead, or how techniques can be adapted.

> Example: "What do you like about this? What do you not like? How can we make this more useful for you?"

11. Ask clients to provide concrete examples of situations in which strategies or skills can be applied.

> Example: "Can you think of a time last week when your children did that?"

12. Offer a cluster of options so the client can choose a course of action from among alternatives.

> Examples:
>   "Let me describe a couple of possibilities, and you tell me which of these makes the most sense for you."
>   "Now that we've gone over different ways that you can figure out whether your beliefs are serving you, which of them will work when you track your beliefs for homework?"
>   "We have talked about many ways you can provide reinforcement for your child's good behavior—a token economy, giving him praise, allowing him to play video games after he does a chore or finishes his homework. Which ones would you be most comfortable with?"

13. Discuss topics in normative terms (e.g., other clients, normative data).

> Example: "I have another parent I'm working with. She was waiting all week to give her children their reward, but then she realized that a week was too long, and they were too young to remember what they were working toward." (Azar & Ferraro, 2000)

14. Use adult analogies to help parents understand information. Selekman (1999) uses an exercise with parents in which they are asked to list the characteristics of their best and worst supervisor. From this exercise, parents often see the importance of praise and reward, and the problems with criticism, yelling, and physical punishment.

15. Validate frustration with new material.

> Example: "This is a lot to take in, but you're doing great."

16. Reframe the time and effort investment in learning new skills.

> Example: "Although it does take work to learn something new, it pays off down the road when you know what to do to keep your children in line. Then you won't have to work as hard and get as stressed out."

17. Reinforce people extensively for their ideas, effort, and achievement. As you already know, reinforcement is a central aspect of behavior theory. It is used as an intervention to increase the likelihood that people will continue to make efforts toward change.

> Examples:
> "You did a good job"
> "I liked the way you said that."
> "You've put a lot of thought into this."
> "You've got a good plan."
> "You've managed to cope with a lot."

18. Work with the client in brief time periods more frequently. In contrast to a social worker in a therapist role, a social worker in a hospital, child welfare, or other crisis-oriented setting sometimes has briefer chunks of time to spend with clients and can be more flexible about the number of contacts.

19. If a client starts to resist the material, make a reflecting statement, and allow him or her to explore feelings and concerns about the approach.

> Example:
> **Client:** I don't know how this is going to help when I have so much going on right now.
> **Social Worker:** You feel overwhelmed, and you're not sure how relevant this is right now.

20. When people insist that they have just "made up their minds" to change a behavior and don't need to learn new behaviors to help them, there are several tactics to take:
    1) Compliment the person on his or her resolve: "I think it's great that you are able to be so committed to your decision to stop using drugs. How are you able to do that?"
    2) Explore what has helped before during times when the client had control over the problem in the past (DeJong & Berg, 2012).

> Examples:
> "How were you able to do that?"
> "What strategies did you use?"
> "What strengths and resources did you draw on?"
> "What did you tell yourself?"
> "What supports did you have in place?"

    3) Relay feedback in normative terms.

> Example: "Most people find that they need some new skills in place for those days when they are stressed out or things don't work out, so they are prepared for times when a sudden urge may catch them by surprise."

21. Involve all family members as necessary in the intervention from the start. In cases of child problems, all adult household members should be included, as well as anyone else that provides a significant amount of care to the child. Obviously, if only one caregiver is implementing the behavioral plan and others are not, the plan will not work. It is not necessary, however, for a child to attend the session; indeed, some research (Lundahl, 2006) indicates that involving only parents may be more effective. See Table 10.1 for ways in which to engage parents.

22. Employ frequent modeling and behavioral rehearsal. (The procedures for role-playing are detailed in Chapter 11.)

23. If people talk about "not feeling motivated" or being "not ready," talk about how thoughts and behaviors are sometimes easier to change than feelings. Additionally, feelings of motivation often change as a result of working on thoughts and behaviors (Beck, 2005).

In order to apply these guidelines for delivering information on new behaviors and skills, read the case in Exercise 10.3 and complete Exercise 10.4.

EXERCISE 10.3: APPLICATION OF GUIDELINES

Exercise Instructions: Examine each guideline and apply it to the case presented here, involving Jaimie, a 15-year-old Latina who is in the juvenile justice system. Her grandmother, Mrs. Valencia, has custody over Jaimie, but Mrs. Valencia's adult son and Jaimie's father, Mr. Cordova, also lives in the home, along with Mrs. Valencia's other adult son, Stephen. Mr. Cordova is physically disabled and has a brain injury.

Social Work Intern: What has been happening with Jamie that has led us to this meeting today?

Mrs. Valencia: Jamie has been missing a lot of school, so she was charged with truancy and now we have to deal with probation.

Social Work Intern: What do you think is the cause of Jamie missing school so much?

Mrs. Valencia: Her brother Steve has violent rages late at night, and it keeps everyone in the house up.

Social Work Intern: Can you describe what you mean by violent rages?

Mrs. Valencia: He screams and throws things. He is usually in the kitchen and banging pots and pans. I don't know what makes him do it.

Social Work Intern: How often is this happening?

Mrs. Valencia: I don't know. It depends on what is happening at home during the week.

Social Work Intern: So, it doesn't happen every night?

Mrs. Valencia: No.

Social Work Intern: What else could be causing Jamie to miss school? She is late everyday, so there has to be more than just Steve's rages on occasion.

Mrs. Valencia: She stays up late every night. She talks to and texts people on her phone, sometimes until two or three in the morning.

(continued)

Social Work Intern: I can see how that would make her too tired to go to school the next day. What have you done to stop her from doing that?

Mrs. Valencia: Nothing. I tried to take away her phone, but she just took mine and used it. When I told her to give my phone back, she hid it.

Mr. Cordova: I've tried to talk to her too, but she refuses to give up her phone or give my mom back hers.

Social Work Intern: Are there any other issues you can think of that keep her from getting to school?

Mrs. Valencia: She is so worried about her appearance that she refuses to go to school until her hair and makeup are just right. She will take a couple of hours blow drying and straightening her hair. Then if it isn't perfect, she refuses to go to school. I wake her up at 4:30 to get ready on time and she will get ready, then go back to sleep, so she misses school. I leave at 5:30, so I can't keep waking her up to make sure she goes.

Social Work Intern: So it seems the main reason she isn't getting to school is because she isn't getting enough sleep. One reason this is happening is because she stays up using her phone until early in the morning. Let's focus on this.

What if you were to take her phone each night and give it back the next morning, only if she is on time for school.

Mrs. Valencia: I don't know what we can do. I've tried to get her to give it to me, but she won't. Plus, I leave for work early, so my son would have to be the one responsible for either giving it back or not.

Social Work Intern: Let's look first at the fact that she may not give it to you. Mrs. Valencia, it is your house and you need to regain control of it. Just because she doesn't want to give it to you, doesn't mean she doesn't have to. Say she doesn't give it to you, what is another way to take away her phone?

Mr. Cordova: We could disconnect the service.

Social Work Intern: I think that's a great idea, Mr. Cordova. Is that something you are willing to do, Mrs. Valencia, if she refuses to give you the phone?

Mrs. Valencia: I did that once before and she just took my phone and refused to give it back.

Social Work Intern: Then I would recommend the same thing for your phone. Disconnect the service.

Mrs. Valencia: I guess I could try that. She will be really upset. I don't know if I could handle the tantrums she will throw.

Social Work Intern: The first thing to do is to sit down with Jamie, together with Mr. Cordova, and explain the changes that will take place. She needs to understand your expectations of her and the consequences for failing to meet those expectations. Mr. Cordova, it will be up to you to ensure that this is consistent. If she isn't on time for school, she absolutely cannot have her phone back.

(continued)

Mrs. Valencia: I could tell her that phones go off at a certain time, and she would need to turn hers off.

Social Work Intern: That's a good idea. What if she doesn't turn it off? Or what if she turns it off, but once you go to bed, she turns it back on?

Mrs. Valencia: I guess I would have to take it from her. But I think this would be better than just taking it from her the first night.

Social Work Intern: I think it's a good step to ease her into the new plan of no phones at night. So, now that we have identified a solution to help Jamie get to sleep sooner, we need to create a goal and objectives that will help you see the results you want and get Jamie to school on time and on a regular basis.

Mrs. Valencia: I definitely cannot be responsible for giving her the phone back if we have to take it away, since I leave for work at 5:30 in the morning.

Social Work Intern: I understand. What could you be responsible for in the plan, Mrs. Valencia?

Mrs. Valencia: I could be the one to take away the phone.

Social Work Intern: Do you have a set time you think would be best to take away her phone?

Mrs. Valencia: I usually go to bed around 10:00, so I think this would be a good time to take it.

Social Work Intern: I think 10:00 is a good time to do that. Mr. Cordova, what is your role in this plan?

Mr. Cordova: I will be the one responsible for giving her back her phone.

Social Work Intern: Do you remember the stipulations we identified for her to get her phone back?

Mr. Cordova: She gets it back if she is on time for school.

Social Work Intern: That's right, but that means she doesn't get it back if she gets in the car on time. She has to be at the school on time, and then you can give her the phone.

Mr. Cordova: I understand.

Social Work Intern: The other point, Mr. Cordova, is if she doesn't go to school at all, she does not get her phone back for the entire day.

Mr. Cordova: She'll get really mad if she doesn't get her phone back.

Social Work Intern: The point of this is to show her that by getting to school on time, she is rewarded with her phone, but if she doesn't go, then she loses it. It's using positive reinforcement for good choices and punishment for poor choices. Regardless of the reason, she is choosing not to go to school. The key to this plan is consistency. You must do what you say you are going to do, and you must mean it. One time of giving in to her and she wins. She'll have control again, and you'll be fighting this battle all the time. Does that make sense?

(continued)

At the next meeting, Mrs. Valencia stated that she and Mr. Cordova had not been consistent in addressing the phone issue with Jamie. She had taken the phone a few times, but Jamie had not gone to school on time, and Mr. Cordova gave her back the phone anyway.

Social Work Intern: If you are not consistent in taking away the phone, then she has no need to start behaving better.

Mrs. Valencia: I know, but even if I take the phone away, my son just gives it back to her in the morning because he doesn't like to upset her.

Social Work Intern: Let's try this again for two more weeks. Maybe we should look at you being the only one implementing this plan, and that way Jamie doesn't get her phone back until the afternoon. The school has asked her not to bring it to school anyway.

Mrs. Valencia: She will not do it. I'm tired of being the bad guy and having her dad go against what I say. I don't want to have to be the only one doing this.

Social Work Intern: I can understand that it's frustrating feeling like you have no support. I'm going to see Jamie at school tomorrow and talk to her about changing her routine for showering and getting ready. I think if she showers at night, then it will help calm her down so she can sleep and then she'll be able to spend less time in the morning getting ready. Are you willing to continue trying to help by taking away the phone at night?

Mrs. Valencia: I will try again, but I don't think I can keep it all day. I will talk to my son about not giving it to her unless she is on time for school.

EXERCISE 10.4: APPLYING GUIDELINES

Exercise Instructions: Complete the chart by applying the guidelines to the case in Exercise 10.3.

Guideline	Application
Explore clients' situations and their feelings before launching into the provision of information.	
Ask the client's permission for you to offer more information.	

(continued)

Guideline	Application

Avoid the use of technical explanations.

What has the person already tried? (previous problem-solving attempts)

Once you have offered information and have discussed it with the client, illicit the client's views on how he or she might use information you have provided.

Ask clients about their knowledge of a particular topic and how it applies to them.

Employ physical and concrete prompts, such as writing tasks or steps down, or having clients place signs in high-traffic areas in the home as reminders of new skills.

Ask deductive questions so that clients can make their own connections and form their own conclusions.

Pay attention to clients' verbal and nonverbal cues. These might include lack of eye contact, one-word responses, yawning, hostile stares, or a rigid posture with arms folded across the chest.

Ask people to describe the skill in their own words.

Elicit clients' reactions to the material. ("What do you think about these ideas?")

When people complain about techniques seeming artificial or "not like life really is," reassure them about the discomfort associated with change and trying out new behaviors until they become a habit. Ask about any adaptations that can be made to make the new behavior feel like it is more within their comfort zone.

Ask clients to provide concrete examples of situations in which strategies or skills can be applied.

Offer a cluster of options so the client can choose among alternatives.

Discuss topics in normative terms.

Use adult analogies to help parents understand information.

Validate frustration with new material.

(continued)

Guideline	Application
Reframe the time and effort investment in learning new skills.	
Compliment people extensively: "You did a good job," or "I liked the way you said that."	
Work with the client in brief time periods more frequently.	
If a client starts to resist the material, make a reflecting statement and explore. If necessary, switch to motivational interviewing or another problem that has higher priority for the client.	
When people insist that they have just "made up their minds" to change a behavior and don't need to learn new behaviors to help them, compliment the person on his or her resolve, explore, give feedback in normative terms, and discuss how they were able to change other challenging behaviors in the past.	
Offer rewards to people for following through with skills (e.g., bus tokens and other transportation vouchers, meals at fast-food restaurants, toys for the children, a positive report at the next court date).	
Employ frequent modeling and behavioral rehearsal.	
If a client doesn't seem motivated, ask about the advantages and disadvantages of the problem behavior or not making a change.	

CBT WITH ETHNIC MINORITY CLIENTS

One of the values of social work involves the delivery of services in a way that is culturally competent. The question becomes, then, is CBT as described here adequate for use with people from minority ethnic backgrounds, or does it need adaptation to make it culturally appropriate? This topic has been subject to debate (Parra Cardona et al., 2012). At the same time, there has been some attention to how CBT may need to be adapted for cultural considerations.

Strategies for adapting CBT include having providers with the same ethnicity as that of clients implement the intervention, and using culturally relevant channels, music, food, and

TABLE 10.3: Culturally Sensitive Adaptations of CBT and Examples

Adaptation	Example
Culture matching: having a member from the same culture provide services	African-American facilitators conducted an attributional intervention for African-American youth referred for aggression (Hudley & Graham, 1993).
Language matching	The Parent Management Training-Oregon program was translated into Spanish language with use of Spanish idioms for concepts presented (Cardona et al., 2012)
Consultation with individuals familiar with the client's culture	A booklet was created about stigma related to mental health for African-American consumers, using ideas solicited from this group. These ideas were then incorporated into the publication (Alvidrez, Snowden, & Kaiser, 2010).
Making services accessible and targeted to clients' circumstances	CBT is delivered during home visiting, because of families' transportation and child care needs.
Provision of extra services designed to enhance client retention	Child care can be offered for other children in the home so that the parent can attend sessions. Bus passes or taxi vouchers can also be provided for transportation.
Explicitly incorporating cultural values	Reinforce that cultural values involve *respeto* (respect) and *buena educacion* (good education; wanting children to have higher educational attainment than they had) by using the operant techniques used in the parent management training program (Parra Cardona et al., 2012).
Exploration of people's experiences of racism, prejudice, and discrimination	In a school-based group intervention, a fourth-grade African-American girl talked about wishing she were white so that she would be prettier. The group facilitators explored with her and the other group members perceptions of beauty and their experiences of internalized oppression.
Use culturally relevant channels and settings	A parent training group offered to Latinas was held at the local church in the community.

language (Kong, Singh, & Krishman-Sarin, 2012; Resnicow et al., 2000). Cultural, social, historical, and psychological influences of behaviors may also be considered. Additionally, themes of the ethnic minority experience, such as acculturation stress, poverty, and discrimination, need be explored. If internalized racism is present, this will also need to be addressed. These ideas for cultural and ethnic adaptation of CBT are summarized and presented with examples in Table 10.3.

Some curriculums have been formulated with cultural sensitivity in mind (see Appendix A). Huey and Polo (2008), in particular, detail many interventions for children from ethnic minority backgrounds who have a variety of mental health disorders, including substance use disorder and aggression. Exercise 10.5 provides an opportunity for you to reflect on the diversity of your clients and appropriate use of CBT.

EXERCISE 10.5: CULTURALLY APPROPRIATE ISSUES FOR CBT

What clients do you see that are from diverse backgrounds? Generally, what are some of the presenting problems that they tackle? Which ones are appropriate for CBT? Which ones are not and what social work interventions would you employ instead?

_____

_____

_____

Pick a problem that is appropriate to target for CBT. Do you see a need for the technique to be delivered in a more culturally appropriate way? How would you do that?

_____

_____

_____

CONCLUSION

This chapter has delved into the delivery of instruction and information, critical components of CBT, and how to do this in a collaborative manner that is attuned to social-work values and ethics. One of the values of social work is the ability to work with people from minority cultural and ethnic groups. Ideas for adapting CBT in a way that is culturally responsive were provided, along with recommendations for further resources.

TEST YOUR SKILLS EXERCISE 10.1: COLLABORATIVE SKILLS

1. According to behavioral theorists, the following are reasons parent training may be ineffective EXCEPT?
   a. The parent's motivation to change his or her behavior may be lacking.
   b. The techniques are not used in a way that maximizes success.
   c. Behavioral principles do not work with all children.
   d. No answer fits; these are all reasons why parent training may be ineffective.

(continued)

2. Choose the best response to complete the statement below. Psychoeducation involves:
   a. Mostly the social worker educating the client about a particular topic.
   b. A social worker providing advice on what a client should do in particular situations so that the client has clear instructions.
   c. A social worker examining relevance of a topic for a client, presenting and personalizing information, and seeking to confirm comprehension.
3. You are going to have a collaborative discussion with a parent about the use of punishment in the home. Before you articulate some of the disadvantages of punishment and present an alternative, what might you want to do first? (Choose the best answer.)
   a. Identify that punishment is never an acceptable technique for changing behavior.
   b. Clarify that you prefer to use positive reinforcement.
   c. Elicit the parent's thoughts and beliefs about punishment.
   d. Get the parents to agree that they need to engage in a new behavior.

CHAPTER 11

ROLE-PLAYING AND HOMEWORK

Now that the delivery of information has been discussed, we move to modeling and behavioral rehearsal, known together as *role-playing*. This chapter also covers how to collaboratively set up homework assignments with clients so that they are able to practice and generalize skills to their problems in everyday living.

MODELING

One of the major paradigms of learning theory is that people learn behaviors by watching others engage in them and being reinforced for them (Bandura, 1977). Called *modeling*, it is a pervasive means of learning for children and adolescents. For instance, children may learn to act appropriately in school by seeing classmates being praised for listening to the teacher and criticized for talking while the teacher is lecturing. People may begin using alcohol or acting aggressively because they have seen their parents and other relatives acting this way.

Modeling is used in CBT as a major method to help people with behavior change. By modeling, the practitioner shows the client how to enact a new behavior. The client then practices the new behavior (called *behavioral rehearsal*), receiving supportive feedback and suggestions for its refinement. Role-playing can be enormously helpful in assisting people to practice new behaviors and to generalize them to real life situations. One of the core values of social work is the importance of human relationships. Role-plays help people practice new interpersonal behaviors so that they are more effective at influencing their environment and fostering healthy relationships.

In order to have an effective role-play, the following guidelines from Hepworth et al. (2012) should be considered:

1. Define a problem that has to do with an interactional pattern that the client wants to change. That is, role-playing is useful when the client's problem has to do with an interaction between two or more people.

2. Discuss how the client can handle a difficult interpersonal situation. Provide educate on communication skills, if needed.

3. Give the client a rationale for a role-play:

> "We have talked about how you can handle this situation, but it is actually much more effective if you can practice the behavior. Would you be willing to do a role-play with me? This way you get to practice the new behavior in a safe environment before actually doing it."
>
> *Or*
>
> "If you can practice this here with me, you can try out a new behavior in a safe place and get some of the kinks out before you use it in real life. And don't worry, I will show you what I mean first, so you won't be asked to do anything you haven't seen first. By actually doing it in here, you are much more likely to be able to do it when the situation calls for it, and you'll be that much more prepared."

4. Model the skills so that clients can observe the new behavior first before they have to try it. Clients are often nervous about this because it means that they will be trying out new or uncomfortable behaviors. But you can reassure them that you will be modeling the behavior first.

5. Discuss how the modeling went.

> "What do you think? How was that different from what usually happens or what you thought might happen?"

You can also offer some empathy for the client's situation after assuming his or her role:

> "I see that she can be very persistent in getting you to change your mind. What did I do to make sure she got the message?"

6. Have the client rehearse the new skill. Do the role-play again, this time having the client practice the new behavior as him- or herself. After having taken part in the first phase of the role-play, clients are usually quick to pick up on the new behavior. Sometimes when first asserting themselves in this new role, they may become

emotional and teary as well. If this happens, you can commend them on working through their emotions in the role-play, pointing out that they will be better equipped to handle the situation in real life. The rehearsal process enables the skills that were unclear or that were misunderstood to come to light for clarification. It also enhances the client's confidence that the skill can be generalized to a real-life situation.

7. Process the behavioral rehearsal with the client. Ask the client what it was like to try on the new behavior. Offer compliments on areas that went well and feedback for improvement, if necessary. At this point, the client may be offered another opportunity to rehearse.

Now that you have read the guidelines, Example 11.1 shows a role play that a social work intern did with one of her clients.

EXAMPLE 11.1: ROLE PLAYING

Mr. Thiebold, a midlife African-American man, was getting help from an intern for problems with anger. He discussed that one of the events that makes him angry is when his friends take advantage of him. He mentioned a specific incident about a friend having borrowed money that he had not paid back.

The intern and the client first talked about the difference between aggression on one side of the equation and passivity on the other, and that assertiveness, or making one's needs known without infringing on the rights of others, was the goal in the middle. She then invited Mr. Thiebold to do a role-play with her on this type of situation. First, she played Mr. Thiebold while he assumed the position of the friend who was withholding payment of his money.

Mr. Thiebold as His Friend: Hey T., it turns out I have other people I have to pay first, so I can't give you the money I owe you this week. You know things have been hard for me, so I hope you'll understand. I'll try to pay you from my next paycheck.

Intern in the Role of Mr. Thiebold: Well, I don't know how to tell you this but I have to be honest with you about the money situation. I lent you the money over a month ago and you have managed to come up with excuses every week, even though you said you'd pay me back right away. If this continues, I'm going to lose trust in you and our friendship might suffer as a result. So I would like you to start paying me right away. If you want, to make things easier for you, we can come up with a payment plan that will allow you to pay me over time in increments.

Mr. Thiebold as His Friend: Oh, I didn't know this was the way you felt. I really didn't realize what I was doing to you. I didn't mean to put others before you and I value our friendship. I appreciate you giving me more time and the payment plan should work well. I'll give you the first payment right away.

(continued)

Mr. Thiebold then played himself with the intern complimenting him afterward during their processing of the role-play.

Social Work Intern: You see how that played out Mr. Thiebold? You did really well asserting yourself to get what you want. Your friend didn't react negatively to it, and the situation got resolved. How did that feel?

Mr. Thiebold: That felt really good. I usually let things happen to me and pass it off with laughter, when deep inside it really hurts me, and then I feel angry at the person and later blow up at them, or mask the feelings with alcohol.

Now use Exercise 11.1 to practice putting together a role-play for a client of your own.

EXERCISE 11.1: ROLE-PLAY

Consider a client whose presenting problem had to do with relationships and supports. Discuss how you would address each aspect of a role-play if you were to do one with that client.

1. Define a problem that has to do with communication in a relationship:

2. Explore and discuss with the client ways of handling the situation. Provide education on effective communication, if needed.

3. Provide rationale for the role-play.

4. Provide modeling.

5. Process modeling.

6. Behavioral rehearsal.

7. Process the behavioral rehearsal.

HOMEWORK

One of the critical methods of CBT is for clients to not only learn new skills in session but also to practice new skills on their own and apply them to their problem behaviors. Therefore, an early part of education about CBT is the importance of homework. An ongoing aspect of the work will also be seeking and securing client buy-in, monitoring homework, and ensuring compliance. Table 11.1 outlines some guidelines for constructing homework with clients (Beck, 2005). Exercise 11.2 provides some practice in using these guidelines.

FOLLOWING THROUGH WITH HOMEWORK

Although ideas, goals, and tasks may have been determined with client input, you should not be surprised to find that clients may not follow through with agreed-upon plans. Consider how hard it is to change our own behavior, such as overeating, watching too much TV, being

---

TABLE 11.1: **Guidelines for Constructing Homework**

1. If necessary, change the label of "homework" to something the client can buy into ("self-help plan," "wellness plan," or "experiment").
2. Provide a rationale for how homework will help in the service of goals that have been established.
3. Suggest "easy" assignments so that clients can motivate and organize themselves to complete them.
4. Ask for input: "What would be most helpful for you to try on your own or work on this week out of all the things we talked about today?"
5. Provide the amount of time it will take: "It will probably take about one minute to jot down your thoughts when your stomach is upset or when you can't sleep."
6. Write down the assignment.
7. Ask clients how likely they are to complete the assignment. Beck (2005) suggests that nothing less than 90% signals that the client will not do it.
8. Role-play if at least part of the homework involves an interaction with another person.
9. Discuss obstacles: "What could get in the way of your doing this?"
10. Elicit thoughts that can get in the way ("I'm too tired") and then discuss ways to counteract them.
11. Have the client summarize what has been agreed upon.

EXERCISE 11.2: CONSTRUCTING HOMEWORK

Consider a client whose presenting problem you are working on with CBT. Go through the guidelines offered and discuss how you would use each of the guidelines in constructing homework with the client.

(continued)

messy, or procrastinating about completing assignments. We may start out with the best of intentions, only to have them dissolve in the face of stressful situations, temptation, or simply the effort it takes to move out of a familiar pattern of behavior.

When clients fail to follow through, we can still maintain a collaborative stance rather than lecturing, scolding, or shaming them. You can explore with the client, in a neutral and nonjudgmental manner, the reasons for the lack of follow-through. Being nonjudgmental does not mean failing to address the client's behavior or letting it go, by saying, "Oh, it's okay." This would give the message that the work you have helped them with is unimportant, and the client might lose motivation and become similarly dismissive.

Instead, at the next contact with the client, inquire about the completion of the task, spending at least five minutes discussing the outcome to emphasize the importance of following through on what was decided (Carroll, 1998). If a person was unable to do the assigned task, time should be spent discussing what got in the way and negotiating the task for the following week. It could be, for instance, that the task was too ambitious for the client—that it needs to be broken down into smaller, more manageable pieces. Table 11.2 lists some select questions that you can use as a guide (Webster-Stratton & Herbert, 1993).

There are certain cognitive responses that clients often make when faced with homework and trying out new skills. Beck (2005) suggests eliciting the thoughts and then discussing an alternative perspective that might motivate the client to do agreed-upon homework (see Table 11.3).

TABLE 11.2: Guiding Questions for Client Task Completion

What makes this hard for you to do?
What can you do to make it easier for you to complete the assignment this week?
What assignment might be more useful for you?
What thoughts come to mind when you think about this assignment?
How could we make this more helpful?

Thoughts that Get in the Way of Follow-Through	Responses
"I don't have the energy to do this."	"It's probably going to take only a minute to do it."
"I don't feel like doing this" or "I'm too tired, I'm not motivated, I don't want to get out of bed."	"I know I don't feel like doing this, but it's important to do it, even if only for five minutes. I can do anything for five minutes. Not doing it makes me feel like I'm too helpless to get better. It's easier to take some action than to wait until I have more energy. I will feel more motivated AFTER I have started."
"Doing these things won't help" or "It's just a drop in the bucket."	"I'm taking action to helping myself feel better and meet my goals." "If I don't do something different, I can't expect that my life will be different." "These small actions will add up. What's important to focus on is that I am building a skill that will serve me in many situations, which will help me over time."

Source: Beck (2005)

EXERCISE 11.3: WHEN CLIENTS DON'T FOLLOW THROUGH

Think about a situation in which a client has not followed through with an agreed-upon task. Lead the client through the process described here and consider what the client might come up with regarding certain cognitive messages that block practice with new skills. How would you respond to these?

Client cognitive messages about homework:

Exploration of responses:

Sometimes clients have homework tasks that involve talking to another person about an uncomfortable topic. In these situations, additional role-playing can help ease anxieties, and the client may feel better ready to commit to the task in person. At the end of this discussion, the client can either commit to the previously agreed-upon task or the task can be renegotiated, if necessary. In any case, the client should summarize the homework, so it is clear that understanding has been reached. After having reviewed this material, use Exercise 11.3 to practice the process of responding to a client who doesn't follow through with doing their homework.

CONCLUSION

The aim of this chapter has been to continue discussion of how CBT techniques are delivered. While the topic of Chapter 10 was psychoeducation, this one explores role-playing and gaining client compliance with homework. Both of these methods focus on getting clients to generalize new information to application in their lives. Role-playing is important when client problems can be improved through better communication with others. Homework—setting it up initially with the client and seeing that clients practice new skills, such as communication—is part of the ongoing work in the direction of positive change.

TEST YOUR SKILLS EXERCISE 11.1: COLLABORATIVE SKILLS

1. _____ is a very important strategy in CBT, as it allows clients to practice their skills with others and rehearse how new behaviors apply to interactions in relationships.
   a. Role-playing
   b. Reinforced learning
   c. Active dialogue
   d. Dynamic transmission
2. Role-playing is appropriate in the following situations EXCEPT:
   a. A woman wants to express her feelings to her partner who is emotionally abusive toward her.
   b. A man is exploring the beliefs that feed into his anger control problem.
   c. A parent is taught how to talk to her teenager about risk-taking.
   d. A woman with an alcohol problem is taught how to resist when others drink.

APPENDIX A

CBT Resources for Child and Adolescent Problems

DEPRESSION

DEPRESSION TREATMENTS FOR ADOLESCENTS

Clarke, G. N., Lewinsohn, P. M., & Hops, H. (1999). *Adolescent coping with depression course*. Portland, OR: Kaiser Permanente. Available online only. Retrieved from http://www.kpchr.org/research/public/acwd/acwd.html

Curry, J, F., Wells, K. C., Brent, D. A., Clarke, G. N., Rohde, P., Albano, A. M., et al. (2005). *Treatment for adolescents with depression study (TADS). Cognitive behavior therapy manual*. Durham, NC: Duke University Medical Center, The TADS Team. Retrieved from https://trialweb.dcri.duke.edu/tads/tad/manuals/TADS_CBT.pdf

Rosselló, J., & Bernal, G, (2007). *Treatment manual for cognitive behavioral therapy for depression. Adaptation for Puerto Rican adolescents*. Center for Psychological Services and Research University of Puerto Rico, Río Piedras. Retrieved from http://ipsi.uprrp.edu/pdf/manuales_tara/individual_manual_eng.pdf

DEPRESSION IN CHILDREN

SELF-CONTROL THERAPY is a school-based group intervention for young elementary-aged children.

Stark, K. D., Reynolds, W. M., & Kaslow, N. J. (1987). A comparison of the relative efficacy of self-control therapy and behavior problem-solving therapy for depression in children. *Journal of Abnormal Child Psychology, 15*, 91–113.

THE PENN PREVENTION PROGRAM (Gillham & Reivich, 1999), also called *The Penn Resiliency Program* is a school-based group intervention for 10- to 15-year-old children. The two main components of the intervention are cognitive (cognitive restructuring and attribution retraining) and social problem solving (problem solving as well as teaching coping strategies for family conflict and other stressors). Accessed online at: http://www.ppc.sas.upenn.edu/prpsum.htm

Gillham, J. F., & Reivich, K. J. (1999). Prevention of depressive symptoms in school children: A research update. *Psychological Science, 10,* 461–462.

PASCET: PRIMARY AND SECONDARY CONTROL ENHANCEMENT TRAINING PROGRAM

Weisz, J. R., Weersing, V. R., Valeri, S. M., & McCarty, C.A. (1999). *Therapist's Manual PASCET: Primary and secondary control enhancement training program.* Los Angeles: University of California.

Weisz, J. R., Weersing, V. R., Valeri, S. M., & McCarty, C. A. (1999). *Act and think: Youth practice book for PASCET.* Los Angeles: University of California.

PERVASIVE DEVELOPMENTAL DISORDERS

Applied behavior analysis (ABA), first developed by Lovaas (2002), involves examination of the antecedents of a problem behavior (the event or situation that precedes the behavior) and its consequences (the event or situation that follows the behavior). Any avoidable antecedents for a problem behavior are removed, and desirable behaviors are taught, followed by positive reinforcement for the child's performance. See: http://www.lovaas.com/resources.php.

Lovaas, O. (1981). *Teaching developmentally delayed children: The me book.* Austin, TX: ProEd Paperback.

Lovaas, O. (2002). *Teaching individuals with developmental delays: Basic intervention techniques.* Austin, TX: ProEd Paperback.

Scarpa, A., White, S. W., & Attwood, T. (Eds.). (2013). *CBT for children and adolescents with high-functioning autism spectrum disorders.* New York: Guilford Press.

ANTI-SOCIAL, AGGRESSIVE, AND CONDUCT PROBLEMS

Social Problem-Solving Approaches

Program	Description
Anger control training (Lochman, Barry, & Pardini, 2003)	In weekly group sessions, children discuss vignettes of social encounters with peers and the social cues and possible motives of individuals in the vignettes. Children learn to use problem solving for dealing with anger-provoking social situations, and they practice appropriate social responses and self-statements in response to different problem situations, first by behavioral rehearsal of the situations with feedback for correct responses. Later in treatment, children practice in anger-provoking situations their use of new anger-control strategies.
Problem-solving skills training (PSST) (Kazdin, 2003)	Designed for children ages 7 to 13 years with disruptive behavior, this is a type of social information-processing intervention. Treatment usually consists of 20 to 25 sessions (40–50 minutes each) conducted with the child, with occasional parent contact. In PSST, children are taught problem-solving strategies and encouraged to generalize these strategies to real-life problems. Skills include identifying the problem, generating solutions, weighing pros and cons of each possible solution, making a decision, and evaluating the outcome. Therapists use in-session practice, modeling, role-playing, corrective feedback, social reinforcement, and token response cost to develop the problem-solving skills gradually, beginning with academic tasks and games and moving to more complex interpersonal situations through role-play. Two other versions of this treatment have added practice and parent management training.
Webster-Stratton child problem-solving training Webster-Stratton (2012)	This training involves a videotape program. In over 100 vignettes, young children and fantasy characters (life-size puppets) are posed in a variety of interpersonal situations that may challenge children with oppositional defiant disorder (ODD). Modeled skills involve the use of social skills, conflict resolution, positive attributions, and perspective-taking.

Parent Training Approaches

Title and Author(s)	Description
Parent Management Training Oregon Model (PMTO) (Patterson, Reid, Jones, & Conger, 1975)	Therapists meet individually with the parents of children between ages 3 and 12 years in 10 to 17 hours of treatment.
Helping the Noncompliant Child (McMahon & Forehand, 2003)	This treatment is for preschool and early school-age children (ages 3–8 years) and is administered to parent–child dyads over 10 weekly sessions.

(continued)

The Incredible Years (Webster-Stratton, Reid, & Hammond, 2012)	This series of videotaped treatment programs has modeling theory as its basis. There are three distinct treatment programs—one for parents, one for children, and one for teachers. Behavioral techniques for the parents of children ages 3 to 8 are modeled through brief videotaped vignettes in the context of a discussion group. Discussion revolves around the correct implementation of techniques by involving parents in problem-solving, role-playing, and rehearsal.
Parent–child interaction therapy for oppositional children (Brinkmeyer & Eyberg, 2003)	This parenting skills training program for young children (ages 2–7 years) with disruptive behavior disorders and their parents targets change in parent–child interaction patterns. Families meet for weekly 1-horr sessions for an average of 12 to 16 sessions, during which parents learn two basic interaction patterns. In the child-directed interaction phase of treatment, they learn specific positive attention skills (emphasizing behavioral descriptions, reflections, and labeled praises) and active ignoring skills, which they use in applying differential social attention to positive and negative child behaviors during a play situation. The emphasis in this phase of treatment is on increasing positive parenting and warmth in the parent–child interaction as the foundation for discipline skills introduced in the second phase, the parent-directed interaction phase of treatment. In this second phase, and within the child-directed context, parents learn and practice giving clear instructions to their child when needed and following through with praise or timeout during in vivo discipline situations. Therapists coach the parents as they interact with their child during the treatment sessions, teaching them to apply the skills calmly and consistently in the clinic until they achieve competency and are ready to use the procedures on their own. Parent-directed interaction homework assignments proceed gradually, from brief practice sessions during play to application at just those times when it is necessary for the child to obey.
Triple P-Positive Parenting Program (Sanders, 1999)	This program has different versions (in content, number of sessions, type of provider) depending on the level of need (ranging from prevention to severe behavior problems), but all are based around parent training. Standard Triple P has a maximum of 12 sessions in group, individual, and self-help formats delivered by mental health providers. The Enhanced Triple P includes increasing parenting skills; it also works to target family stressors, such as parental depression or partner relational problems.
1-2-3 Magic: Effective Discipline for Children 2–12 (4th ed.) (Phelan, 2010)	This approach provides strategies for controlling obnoxious behavior in children, encouraging more positive behavior, and strengthening bonds within the family.

ANXIETY

Cognitive-Behavioral Therapy for Anxious This protocol is appropriate for 7-to 16-year-old youths *Children: Treatment Manual* with generalized anxiety disorder, social phobia, or (Kendall & Hedtke, 2006) separation anxiety disorder. Individual and group treatment manuals are available for this intervention,with adaptations for greater involvement by family members.

Kendall, P. C., & Hedtke, K. A. (2006). Cognitive-Behavioral Therapy for Anxious Children: Therapist Manual. Philadephia: Temple University Workbook Publishing.

OCD

March, J. S., & Mulle, K. (1998). *OCD in children and adolescents: A cognitive-behavioral treatment manual.* New York: Guilford Press.

PTSD

Cohen, J., Mannarino, A., & Deblinger, E. (Eds.). (2012). *Trauma-focused CBT for children and adolescents: Treatment applications.* New York: Guilford Press.

Deblinger, E., & Heflin, A. H. (1996). *Treating sexually abused children and their nonoffending parents: A cognitive behavioral approach.* Thousand Oaks, CA: Sage.

Foa, E. B., Keane, T. M., Friedman, M. J., & Cohen, J. A. (2009). *Effective treatments for PTSD: Practice guidelines from the International Society for Traumatic Stress Studies* (2nd ed.). New York: Guilford Press.

SCHOOL REFUSAL

Kearney, C. A., & Albano, A. M. (2000). *When children refuse school: A cognitive-behavioral therapy approach parent workbook.* Boulder, CO: Graywind Publications.

See http://tfcbt.musc.edu for online training on this model.

SOCIAL PHOBIA IN ADOLESCENTS

Hayward, C., Varady, S., Albano A. M., Thienemann, M., Henderson, L., & Schatzberg, A. F. (2000). Cognitive-behavioral group therapy for social phobia in female adolescents: Results of a pilot study. *Journal of the American Academy of Child Adolescent Psychiatry, 39,* 721–734.

To address the needs of African-American youth in school settings, Ginsburg and Drake (2002) adapted cognitive-behavioral group therapy by reducing the length of treatment, altering examples for developmental and cultural sensitivity, and excluding parents from treatment.

Ginsburg, G. S., & Drake, K. L. (2002). School-based treatment for anxious African-American adolescents: A controlled pilot study. *Journal of the American Academy of Child & Adolescent Psychiatry, 41*(7), 768–775.

SOCIAL PHOBIA IN CHILDREN

Beidel, D. C., & Turner, S. M. (1998). *Shy children, phobic adults: Nature and treatment of social phobia.* Washington, DC: American Psychological Association.

Silverman, W. K., & Kurtines, W. M. (1996). *Anxiety and phobic disorders: A pragmatic approach.* New York: Springer.

SUBSTANCE USE DISORDERS IN ADOLESCENTS

Godley, S. H., Meyers, R. J., Smith, J. E., Karvinen, T., Titus, J. C., Godley, M. D., et al. (2008). *The adolescent community reinforcement approach (ACRA) for adolescent cannabis users, Cannabis youth treatment (CYT) series,* Vol. 4. DHHS Publication No. SMA01-3864. Rockville, MD: Center for Substance Abuse Treatment, Substance Abuse and Mental Health Services Administration. Retrieved from http://store.samhsa.gov/ product/The-Adolescent-Community-Reinforcement-Approach-for-Adolescent-Cannabis-Users/ SMA08-3864

This behavioral intervention involves functional analysis and contingencies for sobriety behavior. For more information, see http://www.cebc4cw.org/program/adolescent-community-reinforcement-approach/detailed.

Webb, C., Scudder., M., Kaminer., Y., & Kadden., R. (2008). *Motivational enhancement therapy and cognitive behavioral therapy supplement: Seven sessions of cognitive behavioral therapy for adolescent cannabis users. Cannabis youth treatment (CYT) series,* Vol. 2. DHHS Publication No. SMA08-3954. Rockville, MD: Center for Substance Abuse Treatment, Substance Abuse and Mental Health Services Administration. Retrieved from http:// http://store.samhsa.gov/shin/content//SMA08-3954/SMA08-3954.pdf

GROUP THERAPY FOR CHILDREN

Christner, R. W., Stewart, J. L., & Freeman, A. (Eds.). (2007). *Handbook of cognitive-behavior group therapy with children and adolescents: Specific settings and presenting problems.* New York: Routledge.

For further resources, many more cognitive-behavioral treatments are available on the Society of Clinical Psychology, American Psychological Association, Division 12 Task Force website for evidence-based treatment: http://www.div12.org/PsychologicalTreatments/index.html.

APPENDIX B

Resources: CBT Treatment Manuals for Adults

ADHD

CBT includes education about ADHD, training in organizing and planning, learning skills to reduce distractibility, cognitive restructuring (learning to think more adaptively in situations that cause distress), and relapse prevention.

Safren, S. A., Perlman, C. A., Sprich, S., & Otto, M. W. (2005). *Mastering your adult ADHD: Client workbook. A cognitive behavioral treatment program*. New York: Oxford University Press.

Safren, S. A., Perlman, C. A., Sprich, S., & Otto, M. W. (2005). *Mastering your adult ADHD: Therapist guide. A cognitive behavioral treatment program*. New York: Oxford University Press.

ANGER MANAGEMENT

Reilly, P. M., & Shopshire, M. S. (2008). *Anger management for substance abuse and mental health clients: A cognitive behavioral therapy manual*. DHHS Publication No. SMA13-4213. Rockville, MD: US Department of Health and Human Services, Substance Abuse and Mental Health Services Administration, Center for Substance Abuse Treatment. Retrieved from http:// http://store.samhsa.gov/shin/content// SMA13-4213/SMA13-4213.pdf

ANXIETY

Abramowitz, J. S., Deacon, B. J., & Whiteside, S. P. H. (2011). *Exposure therapy for anxiety: Principles and practice.* New York: Guilford Press.

For treatment manuals for anxiety disorders listed here see: http://www.crufad.org/index.php/treatment-support/treatment-manuals

ACUTE STRESS DISORDER

CBT for acute stress disorder manual. Retrieved from http://www.istss.org/Content/MainNavigationMenu/TreatingTrauma/TreatmentMaterials/CognitiveBehavioralTherapyforAcuteStressDisorderCBTforASD/BryantCBTforASDmanual.pdf

GENERALIZED ANXIETY DISORDER

Andrews, G., Creamer, M., Crino, R., Hunt, C., Lampe, L., & Page, A. (2002). Generalized anxiety disorder. Patient treatment manual. In The treatment of anxiety disorders: Clinician guides and patient manuals (2nd ed.). New York: Cambridge University Press. Retrieved from http://www.crufad.org/images/stories/pdf/manuals/crufad_GADmanual.pdf

OBSESSIVE-COMPULSIVE DISORDER

Andrews, G., Creamer, M., Crino, R., Hunt, C., Lampe, L., & Page, A. (2002). Obsessive-compulsive disorder. Patient treatment manual. In *The treatment of anxiety disorders: Clinician guides and patient manuals* (2nd ed.). New York: Cambridge University Press. Retrieved from http://www.crufad.org/images/stories/pdf/manuals/crufad_OCDmanual.pdf

PANIC DISORDER

Andrews, G., Creamer, M., Crino, R., Hunt, C., Lampe, L., & Page, A. (2002). Anxiety and panic disorder. Patient treatment manual. In *The treatment of anxiety disorders: Clinician guides and patient manuals* (2nd ed.). New York: Cambridge University Press. Retrieved from http://www.crufad.com/images/stories/pdf/manuals/crufad_Panicmanual.pdf

PTSD

Andrews, G., Creamer, M., Crino, R., Hunt, C., Lampe, L., & Page, A. (2002). Posttraumatic disorder. Patient treatment manual. In *The treatment of anxiety disorders: Clinician guides and patient manuals* (2nd ed.). New York: Cambridge University Press. Retrieved from http://www.crufad.org/images/stories/pdf/manuals/crufad_PTSDmanual.pdf

Foa, E. B., Keane, T. M., Friedman, M. J., & Cohen, J. A. (2009). *Effective treatments for PTSD: Practice guidelines from the International Society for Traumatic Stress Studies* (2nd ed.). New York: Guilford.

Andrews, G., Creamer, M., Crino, R., Hunt, C., Lampe, L., & Page, A. (2002). Social phobia. Patient treatment manual. In *The treatment of anxiety disorders: Clinician guides and patient manuals* (2nd ed.). New York: Cambridge University Press. Retrieved from http://www.crufad.org/images/stories/pdf/manuals/crufad_SocialPmanual.pdf

Hofmann, S. G., & Otto, M. W. (2008). *Cognitive behavioral therapy of social phobia: Evidence-based and disorder-specific treatment techniques.* New York: Routledge.

SPECIFIC PHOBIAS

Andrews, G. (1994). *The Treatment of anxiety disorders: clinician guides and patient manuals.* Cambridge: Cambridge University Press.

Andrews, G., Creamer, M., Crino, R., Hunt, C., Lampe, L., & Page, A. (2002). Specific phobias. Patient treatment manual. In *The treatment of anxiety disorders: Clinician guides and patient manuals* (2nd ed.). New York: Cambridge University Press. Retrieved from http://www.crufad.com/images/stories/pdf/manuals/crufad_SpecPhobmanual

DEPRESSION

CBT for depression involves *behavioral* models that focus on the development of coping skills, especially in the domains of social skills and cultivating pleasant daily activities, so that the person receives more reinforcement from his or her environment. *Cognitive* models include assessment and changing of the distorted thinking that people with depression exhibit. Although typically delivered as a package of interventions, some of the techniques have been used as stand-alone treatment. These include behavioral activation treatment, which centers on activity scheduling and increasing pleasant activities, and problem-solving therapy, which focuses on behaviorally defining specific problems, brainstorming ideas to solve them, and deciding on and implementing solutions.

Beck, A. T., Rush, A. J., Shaw, B. F., & Emery, G. (1979). *Cognitive therapy of depression.* New York: Guilford Press.

Lejuez, C. W., Hopko, D. R., & Daughters, S. B. (2004). A mental health counselor's guide to the brief behavioral activation treatment for depression (BATD). In *New Directions in Mental Health Counseling* (pp. 81–90). Long Island City, NY: Hatherleigh.

Muñoz, R., & Miranda, J. (1996). *Individual therapy manual for cognitive-behavioral treatment of depression.* Santa Monica, CA: RAND. Retrieved from http://www.rand.org/content/dam/rand/pubs/monograph_reports/2005/MR1198.6.pdf

Muñoz, R. F., & Miranda, J. (1993). *Group therapy manual for cognitive-behavioral treatment of depression.* Los Angeles: University of California.

HEALTH CONDITIONS

Burgess, M., & Chalder, T. (2004). *Manual for participants: Cognitive behavior therapy for CFS/ME.* Pace Trial Management Group.

Nezu, A. M., & Nezu, C. M. (2010). Cognitive-behavioral case formulation and treatment design. In R. A. DiTomasso, B. A. Golden, & H. J. Morris (Eds.). *Handbook of cognitive-behavioral approaches in primary care* (pp. 201–222). New York: Springer.

MINDFULNESS

Baer, R. A. (Ed). (2006). *Mindfulness-based treatment approaches: Clinician's guide to evidence base and applications.* Boston: Academic Press.

Bowen, S., Chawla, N., & Marlatt, G. A. (2011). *Mindfulness-based relapse prevention for addictive behaviors. A clinician's guide.* New York: Guilford Press.

Lee, M. Y., Ng, S., Leung, P. P. Y., & Chan, C. L. W. (2009). *Integrative body-mind-spirit-social work: An empirically based approach to assessment and treatment.* New York: Oxford University Press.

Roemer, L., & Orsillo, S. M. (2009). *Mindfulness- and acceptance-based behavioral therapies in practice.* New York: Guilford Press.

Segal, Z. V., Williams, J. M. G., & Teasdale, J. D. (2002). *Mindfulness-based cognitive therapy for depression: A new approach to preventing relapse.* New York: Guilford Press.

Williams, J. M. G., Duggan, D. S., Crane, C., & Fennell, M. V. (2006). Mindfulness-based cognitive therapy for prevention of recurrence of suicidal behavior. *Journal of Clinical Psychology, 62,* 201–210.

Williams, J. M. G., Teasdale, J. D., Segal, Z. V., & Kabat-Zinn, J. (2007). *The mindful way through depression: Freeing yourself from chronic unhappiness.* New York: Guilford Press.

OLDER ADULTS

Laidlaw, K., Thompson, L. W., Dick-Siskin, L., &Gallagher-Thompson, D. (2003). *Cognitive behaviour therapy with older people.* Chichester, UK: Wiley.

PERSONALITY DISORDERS

Sperry, L. (2006). *Cognitive behavior therapy of DSM-IV-TR personality disorders: Highly effective interventions for the most common personality disorders* (2nd ed.). New York: Routledge.

SUBSTANCE USE DISORDERS

Budney, A. J., & Higgins, S. T. (1998). *Therapy manuals for drug addiction: A community reinforcement approach: Treating cocaine addiction.* National Institute on Drug Abuse NIH Publication Number 98-4309. Retrieved from http://www.nida.nih.gov/TXManuals/CRA/CRA1.html

Kadden, R., Carrol, K., Donovan, D., Cooney, N., Monti, P., Abrams, D., Litt, M., & Hester, R, (Eds). (2003). *Cognitive behavioral coping skills therapy manual: A clinical research guide for therapists treating individuals with alcohol abuse and dependence. Project MATCH,* Vol. 3. NIH Publication No. 94-3724. Bethesda,

MD: National Institutes of Health, Public Health Service. Retrieved from http://pubs.niaaa.nih.gov/publications/MATCHSeries3/Project%20MATCH%20Vol_3.pdf

SOCIAL WORK

Cormier, L. S., Nurius, P., & Osborn, C. J. (2009). *Interviewing and change strategies for helpers: Fundamental skills and cognitive behavioral interventions* (6th ed.). Belmont, CA: Brooks/Cole.

Ronen, T., & Freeman, A. (Eds.). (2007). *Cognitive behavior therapy in clinical social work practice.* New York: Springer.

Cully, J. A., & Teten, A. L. (2008). *A therapist's guide to brief cognitive behavioral therapy.* Houston, TX: Department of Veterans Affairs South Central MIRECC. Retrieved from http://www.mirecc.va.gov/visn16/docs/therapists_guide_to_brief_cbtmanual.pdf

OTHER CBT RESOURCES

Barlow, D. H. (Ed.). (2008). *Clinical handbook of psychological disorders* (4th ed.). New York: Guilford Press.

Beck, J. S. (2005). *Cognitive therapy for challenging problems: What to do when the basics don't work.* New York: Guilford Press.

Many more cognitive-behavioral treatments are available on the Society of Clinical Psychology, American Psychological Association, Division 12 Task Force website for evidence-based treatment: http://www.div12.org/PsychologicalTreatments/index.html

REFERENCES

Abramson, L. Y., Metalsky, G. I., & Alloy, L. B. (1989). Hopelessness depression: A theory-based subtype of depression. *Psychological Review, 96*(2), 358–372.

Alvidrez, J., Snowden, L. R., & Kaiser, D. M. (2010). Involving consumers in the development of a psychoeducational booklet about stigma for black mental health clients. *Health Promotion Practice, 11*(2), 249–258.

Armelius, B., & Andreassen, T. H. (2007). Cognitive-behavioral treatment for antisocial behavior in youth in residential treatment. *Cochrane Developmental, Psychosocial and Learning Problems Group.*

Azar, S. T., Barnes, K. T., & Twentyman, C. T. (1988). Developmental outcomes in physically abused children: Consequences of parental abuse or the effects of a more general breakdown in caregiving behaviors? *Behavior Therapist, 11*, 27–32.

Azar, S. T., & Ferraro, M. (2000). How can parenting be enhanced? In In H. Dubowitz & D. DePanfilis (Eds.), *Handbook for child protection practice* (pp. 437–624). Thousand Oaks, CA: Sage Publications.

Bandura, A. (1977). *Social learning theory.* Englewood Cliffs, NJ: Prentice-Hall.

Bannick, F. (2012). *Practising positive CBT: From reducing distress to building success.* Chichester: Wiley-Blackwell.

Barber, J. G., & Gilbertson, R. (1997). Unilateral interventions for women living with heavy drinkers. *Social Work, 42*, 69–78.

Beck, A. T. (1976). *Cognitive therapy and the emotional disorders.* New York: International Universities Press.

Beck, A. T., & Freeman, A. (1990). *Cognitive therapy and depression.* New York: Guilford Press.

Beck, J. S. (2011). *Cognitive therapy: Basics and beyond* (2nd ed.). New York: Guilford Press.

Beck, J. S. (2005). *Cognitive therapy for challenging problems: What to do when the basics don't work.* New York: Guilford Press.

de Jong, P. & Berg, I. K. (2012). *Interviewing for solutions* (4th ed.). Belmont, CA: Cengage Learning.

Bernandy, K. Füber, N., Köllner, V., & Häuser, W. (2010). Efficacy of cognitive-behavioral therapies in fibromyalgia syndrome—a systematic review and metaanalysis of randomized controlled trials. *The Journal of Rheumatology, 37*(10), 1991–2005.

Briere, J., & Elliot, D. (2003). Prevalence and psychological sequelae of self-reported childhood physical and sexual abuse in a general population sample of men and women. *Child Abuse and Neglect, 27*(10), 1205–1222.

Carroll, K. (1998). *A cognitive-behavioral approach: Treating cocaine addiction.* Retrieved from http://www.drugabuse.gov/TXManuals/CBT/CBT1.html

Chambless, D. L., & Hollon, S. D. (1998). Defining empirically supported therapies. *Journal of Consulting and Clinical Psychology, 66*(1), 7–18.

Chorpita, B. F., Becker, K. D., & Daleiden, E. L. (2007). Understanding the common elements of evidence-based practice: Misconceptions and clinical examples. *Journal of American Academy of Child and Adolescent Psychiatry, 46*(5), 647–652.

Christensen, D. N., Todahl, J., & Barrett, W. G. (1999). *Solution-based casework: An introduction to clinical and case management skills in casework practice.* New York, NY: Aldine DeGruyter.

Clarke, G. N., Lewinsohn, P. M., & Hops, H. (1999). *Adolescent coping with depression course.* Portland, OR: Kaiser Permanente. Available online only. Retrieved from http://www.kpchr.org/research/public/acwd/acwd.html

Connors, G., Donovan, D., & DiClemente, C. (2001). *Substance abuse treatment and stages of change: Selecting and planning interventions.* New York: Guilford Press.

Corcoran, J. (2011). *Mental health treatment for children and adolescents.* New York: Oxford University Press.

Corcoran, K. & Fisher, J. (Eds.). (2013). *Measures for clinical practice and research: A sourcebook* (5th ed.) (Vols. 1–2). New York: Oxford University Press.

Corcoran, J., & Ivery, J. (2004). Parent and child attributions for child behavior: Distinguishing factors for engagement and outcome. *Families in Society, 85*(1), 101–106.

Cordova, J. V. (2001). Acceptance in behavior therapy: Understanding the process of change. *The Behavior Analyst, 24*(2), 213–226.

Cordova, A., & Jacobson, N. (2001). Couple distress. In D. Barlow (Ed.), *Clinical handbook of psychological disorders: A step-by-step treatment manual* (3rd ed.). New York: Guilford Press. *Behavior Modification, 17,* 407–457.

Cormier, L. S., Nurius, P., & Osborn, C. J. (2009). *Interviewing and change strategies for helpers: Fundamental skills and cognitive behavioral interventions* (6th ed.). Belmont, CA: Brooks/Cole.

Cournoyer, B. (2010). *The social work skills workbook.* Pacific Grove, CA: Brooks/Cole.

Creed, T. A., Reisweber, J., & Beck, A. T. (2011). *Cognitive therapy for adolescents in school settings.* New York: Guilford Press.

Deblinger, E., & Heflin, A. H. (1996). *Treating sexually abused children and their nonoffending parents: A cognitive-behavioral approach.* Thousand Oaks, CA: Sage.

DeJong, P., & Berg, I. K. (2012). *Interviewing for solutions* (2nd ed.). Pacific Grove, CA. Brooks/Cole.

Dissanayake, R. K., & Bertouch, J. V. (2010). Psychosocial interventions as adjunct therapy for patients with rheumatoid arthritis: A systematic review. *International Journal of Rheumatoid Diseases, 13,* 324–334.

Dobson, K., & Dozois, D. (2001). Historical and philosophical bases of the cognitive-behavioral therapies. In K. Dobson (Ed.), *Handbook of cognitive-behavioral therapies* (2nd ed., pp. 3–39). New York: Guilford Press.

D'Zurilla, T., & Nezu, A. (2010). Problem-solving therapies. In K. Dobson (Ed.), *Handbook of cognitive-behavioral therapies* (3rd ed., pp. 197–225). New York: Guilford Press.

Early, T. J., & Newsome, W. S. (2005). Measures for assessment and accountability in practice with families from a strengths perspective. In J. Corcoran (Ed.), *Building strengths and skills: A collaborative approach to working with clients* (pp. 359–394). New York: Oxford University Press.

Ellis, A., & McLaren, C. (1998). *Rational emotive behavior therapy: A therapist's guide* (Vol. 2.). Atascadero, CA: Impact Publishers.

Emery, G. (1985). Cognitive therapy: Techniques and applications. In A. T. Beck & G. Emery (Eds.), *Anxiety disorders and phobias: A cognitive perspective* (pp. 167–313). New York: Basic Books.

Feindler, E. (2009). Playful strategies to manage frustration: The turtle technique and beyond. In A. A. Drew (Ed.), *Blending play therapy with cognitive behavioral therapy: Evidence-based and other effective treatments and techniques* (p. 401). Hoboken, NJ: Wiley.

Foa, E. B., Keane, T. M., Friedman, M. J., & Cohen, J. A. (2009). *Effective treatments for PTSD: Practice guidelines from the International Society for Traumatic Stress Studies* (2nd ed.). New York: Guilford Press.

Forehand, R., & Kotchick, B. A. (1996). *Cultural diversity: A wake-up call for parent training. Behavior Therapy, 27,* 187–206.

Fors, E. A., Bertheussen, G. F., Thune, I., Juvet, L. K., Elvsaas, I. K., Oldervoll, L., Anker, G.,...Leviseth, Gunnar. (2010). Psychosocial interventions as part of breast cancer rehabilitation programs? Results from a systematic review. *Psycho-Oncology, 20*(9), 909–918.

Freeman, W. S., Johnston, C., & Barth, F. M. (1997). Parent attributions for inattentive-overactive, oppositional-defiant, and prosocial behaviours in children with attention deficit hyperactivity disorder. *Canadian Journal of Behavioural Science, 29*(4), 239–248.

Gershoff, E. T. (2002). Corporal punishment by parents and associated child behaviors and experiences: A meta-analytic and theoretical review. *Psychological Bulletin, 128*(4), 539–579.

Gershoff, E. T., Lansford, E. L., Sexton, H. R., Davis-Kean, P., Sameroff, A. J. (2012). Longitudinal links between spanking and children's externalizing behaviors in a national sample of White, Black, Hispanic, and Asian American Families. *Child Development, 83*(3), 838–843.

Gilbert, R., Widom, C. S., Browne, K., Webb, E., & Janson, S. (2009). Burden and consequences of child maltreatment in high-income countries. *The Lancet, 373*(9657), 68–81.

Gotlib, I., & Abramson, L. (1999). Attributional theories of emotion. In T. Dalgleish & M. Power (Eds.), *Handbook of cognition and emotion* (pp. 613–636). New York: John Wiley & Sons.

Hayes, S. C., Strosahl, K. D., & Wilson, P. K. G. (2011). *Acceptance and commitment therapy: The process and practice of mindful change.* New York: Guilford Press.

Hepworth, D. H., Rooney, R. H., Rooney, G. D., Strom-Gottfried, K., & Larsen, J. A. (2012). *Direct social work practice: Theory and skills.* Pacific Grove, CA: Brooks/Cole Publishing Company.

Hofmann, S. G., Smits, J. A. J. (2008). Cognitive-behavioral therapy for adult anxiety disorders: A meta-analysis of randomized placebo-controlled trials. *Journal of Clinical Psychiatry, 69*(4), 621–632.

Holahan, C. J., Moos, R. H., Holahan, C. K., Brennan P. L., & Schutte K. K., (2005). Stress generation, avoidance coping, and depressive symptoms: a 10-year model. *Journal of Consulting and Clinical Psychology, 73,* 658–666.

Hudley, C., & Graham, S. (1993). An attributional intervention to reduce peer-directed aggression among African-American boys. *Child Development, 64*(1), 124–138.

Huey, S. J. Jr., & Polo, A. J. (2008). Evidence-based psychosocial treatments for ethnic minority youth. *Journal of Clinical Child & Adolescent Psychology, 37*(1), 262–301.

James, A., Soler, A., & Weatherall, R. (2005). Cognitive behavioural therapy for anxiety disorders in children and adolescents. *Cochrane Database of Systematic Reviews, 4.*

Johnson, M. D., Cohan, C. L., Davila, J., Lawrence, E., Rogge, R. D., Karney, B. R., Sullivan, K. T.,...Bradbury, T. N. (2005). Problem-solving skills and affective expressions as predictors of change in marital satisfaction. *Journal of Consulting and Clinical Psychology, 73*(1), 15–27.

Kadzin, A. E. (2003). Psychotherapy for children and adolescents. *Annual review of Psycology, 54*(1), 253–276.

Kazdin, A. (2012). *Behavior modification in applied settings* (7th ed.). Long Grove, IL: Waveland Press.

Karver, M. S., Handelsman, J. B., & Fields, S. (2006). Meta-analysis of therapeutic relationship variables in youth and family therapy: The evidence for different relationship variables in the child and adolescent treatment outcome literature. *Clinical Psychology Review, 26*(1), 50–65.

Kendall, P., Kane, M., Howard, B., & Siqueland, L. (1990). *Cognitive–behavioral therapy for anxious children. Treatment manual.* Admore, PA: Workbook Publishing.

Kliem, S., Kroger, C., & Kosfelder, J. (2010). Dialectical behavior therapy for borderline personality disorder: A meta-analysis using mixed-effects modeling. *Journal of Consulting and Clinical Psychology, 78*(6), 936–951.

Knell, S. M., & Dasari, M. (2009). CBPT: Implementing and integrating CBPT into clinical practice. In A. A. Drewes (Ed.), *Blending play therapy with cognitive behavioral therapy. Evidence-based and other effective treatments and techniques* (pp. 321–352). Hoboken, NJ: Wiley.

Kong, G., Singh, N., & Krishnan-Sarin, S. (2012). A review of culturally targeted/tailored tobacco prevention and cessation interventions for minority adolescents. *Nicotine and Tobacco Research, 14*(12), 1394–1406.

Leahy, R. L. (1996). *Cognitive therapy: Basic principles and applications.* Northvale, NJ: Aronson.

Lee, C., & White, H. R. (2012). Effects of childhood maltreatment on violent injuries and premature death during young adulthood among urban high-risk men. *Archives of Pediatric & Adolescent Medicine, 166*(9), 814–820. DOI:10.1001/archpediatrics.2012.244

Linehan, M. (1993). *Cognitive-behavioral treatment of borderline personality disorder.* New York: Guilford Press.

Lipsey, M. W., Landenberger, N. A., & Wilson, S. J. (2007). Effects of cognitive-behavioral programs for criminal offenders. *Campbell systematic reviews, 6,* 1–27.

Lochman, J. E., Barry, T. D., & Pardini, D. (2003). Anger control training for aggressive youths. In A. E. Kazdin & J. R. Weisz (Eds.), *Evidence-based psychotherapies for children and adolescents* (pp. 263–281). New York: Guilford Publications.

Lovaas, O. (1976). *The autistic child: Language development through behavior modification.* New York: Irvington Publishers; distributed by Halsted Press.

Lovaas, O. (1981). *Teaching developmentally delayed children: The me book.* Austin, TX: ProEd Paperback.

Lovaas, O. (2002). *Teaching individuals with developmental delays: Basic intervention techniques.* Austin, TX: ProEd Paperback.

Lundahl, B., Risser, H. J., & Lovejoy, M. C. (2006). A meta-analysis of parent training: Moderators and follow-up effects. *Clinical Psychology Review, 26*(1), 86–104.

Lynch, T., Chapman, A., Rosenthal, Z. M., Kuo, J. R., & Linehan, M. M. (2006). Mechanisms of change in dialectical behavior therapy: Theoretical and empirical observations. *Journal of Clinical Psychology, 62*(4), 459–480.

Macdonald, G., Higgins, J., & Ramchandani, P. (2006). *Cognitive-behavioural interventions for children who have been sexually abused.* Campbell Collaboration.

Mash, E. J., & Barkley, R. A. (2009). *Assessment of childhood disorders* (4th ed.). New York: Guilford Press.

McCart, M. R., Priester, P. E., Davies, W. H., & Azen, R. (2006). Differential effectiveness of behavioral parent-training and cognitive-behavioral therapy for antisocial youth: A meta-analysis. *Journal of Abnormal Child Psychology, 34*(4), 525–541.

McKay, M., Davis, M., & Fanning, P. (2011). *Thoughts and feelings: Taking control of your moods and your life* (4th ed.). Oakland, CA: New Harbinger Publications.

McMahon, R. J., & Forehand, R. (2003). *Helping the noncompliant child: Family-based treatment for oppositional behavior* (2nd ed.). New York: Guilford Press.

Meichenbaum, D. (1999). *Cognitive-behavior modification: An integrative approach.* Cambridge, MA: Perseus Publishing.

Miller, W. R., & Rollnick, S. (2012). *Motivational interviewing: Helping people change.* New York: Guilford Press.

Moyers, T. B., Martin, T., Houck, J. M., Christopher, P. J., & Tonigan, J. S. (2009). From in-session behaviors to drinking outcomes: A causal chain for motivational interviewing. *Journal of Consulting and Clinical Psychology, 77*(6), 1113–1124.

Murphy, J. (2008). *Solution-focused counseling in middle and high schools* (2nd ed.). Alexandria, VA: American Counseling Association.

Mytton, J., DiGuiseppi, C., Gough, D., Taylor, R., & Logan, S. (2006). School-based secondary prevention programmes for preventing violence. *Cochrane database of systematic reviews, 3.*

National Association of Social Workers. (1997). *Code of Ethics.* Washington, DC: Author.

Noleen-Hoeksema, S. (2002). Gender Differences in depression. In I. Gothlib & C. Hammen (Eds.), *Handbook of Depression* (pp. 492–509). New York: Guilford Press.

Parra Cardona, J. R., Domenech-Rodriguez, M., Forgach, M., Sullivan, C., Bybee, D., Holtrop, K., Escobar-Chew, A. R., ... Bernal, G. (2012). Culturally adapting an evidence-based parenting intervention for Latino immigrants: The need to integrate fidelity and cultural relevance. *Family Process, 51*(1), 56–72.

Patterson, G. R., Reid, J. B., Jones, R. R., & Conger, R. E. (1975). *A social learning theory approach to family intervention: Volume I. Families with aggressive children.* Eugene, OR: Castalia Publishing.

Pavlov, I. P. (1932). Neuroses in man and animals. *Journal of the American Medical Association. 9,* 1012–1013.

Pavlov, I. P. (1934). An attempt at a physiological interpretation of obsessional neurosis and paranoia. *Journal of Mental Science, 80,* 187–197.

Phelan, T. W. (2010). *1-2-3 magic: Effective discipline for children 2–12.* Glen Ellyn, IL: ParentMagic.

Podell, J. L., Martin, E. D., & Kendall, P. C. (2009). Incorporating play within a manual-based CBT treatment for children and adolescents with anxiety disorders. In A. A. Drewes (Ed.), *Blending play therapy with cognitive behavioral therapy: Evidence-based and other effective treatments and techniques* (pp. 165–178). Hoboken, NJ: John Wiley & Sons.

Prochaska, J., & DiClemente, C. (1984). *The transtheoretical approach: Crossing traditional boundaries of therapy.* Malabar, FL: Krieger.

Prochaska, J., & Norcross, J. (1994). *Systems of psychotherapy: A transtheoretical analysis* (3rd ed.). Pacific Grove, CA: Brooks/Cole.

Reilly, P. M., & Shopshire, M. S. (2008). *Anger management for substance abuse and mental health clients: A cognitive behavioral therapy manual.* DHHS Publication No. SMA13-4213. Rockville, MD: US Department of Health and Human Services, Substance Abuse and Mental Health Services Administration, Center for Substance Abuse Treatment. Retrieved from http:// http://store.samhsa.gov/shin/content// SMA13-4213/SMA13-4213.pdf

Resnicow, K., Soler, R., Braithwaite, R. L., Ahluwalia, J. S., & Butler, J. (2000). Development of a racial and ethnic identity scale for African American adolescents: The survey of Black life. *Journal of Black Psychology, 25*(2), 171–188.

Rohde, L. A., Szobot, C., Polanczyk, G., Schmitz, M., Martins, S., & Tramontina, S. (2005): Attention-deficit/ hyperactivity disorder in a diverse culture: Do research and clinical findings support the notion of a cultural construct for the disorder? *Biological Psychiatry 57,* 1436–1441.

Robin, A. L., & Foster, S. L. (2002). *Negotiating parent adolescent conflict: A behavioral family systems approach.* Guilford Press.

Sackett, D. L., Richardson, W. S., Rosenberg, W., & Haynes, R. B. (1997). *Evidence-based medicine: How to practice & teach EBM.* New York: Churchill Livingstone.

Sanders, M. R. (1999). Triple P-Positive Parenting Program: Towards an empirically validated multilevel parenting and family support strategy for the prevention of behavior and emotional problems in children. *Clinical Child and Family Psychology Review, 2*(2), 71–90.

Scarpa, A., White, S. W. & Attwood, T. (Eds.). (2013). *CBT for children and adolescents with high functioning autism spectrum disorders.* New York: Guilford Press.

Selekman, M. (1999). The solution-oriented parenting group revisited. *Journal of Systemic Therapies, 18*(1), 5–23.

Seligman, M. (2011). *Learned optimism.* New York: Knopf.

Shelby, J. S., & Berk, M. S. (2009). Play therapy, pedagogy and CBT: An argument for interdisciplinary synthesis. A. A. Drewes (Ed.), *Blending play therapy with cognitive behavioral therapy: Evidence-based and other effective treatments and techniques* (pp. 17–40). Hoboken, NJ: Wiley.

Sisson, R. W., & Azrin, N. H. (1986). Family-member involvement to initiate and promote treatment of problem drinkers. *Journal of Behavioral Therapy and Experiential Psychiatry, 17,* 15–21.

Skinner, B. F. (1953). *Science and human behavior.* New York: Macmillan.

Smith, C. A., Ireland, T. O., Thornberry, T. P. (2005). Adolescent maltreatment and its impact on young adult antisocial behavior. *Child Abuse & Neglect, 29*(10), 1099–1119. DOI:10.1016/j.chiabu.2005.02.011

Stark, K. D., Reynolds, W. M., & Kaslow, N. J. (1987). A comparison of the relative efficacy of self-control therapy and a behavioral problem-solving therapy for depression in children. *Journal of Abnormal Child Psychology, 15*(1), 91–113.

Stark, K. D., Rouse, L., & Livingston, R. (1991). Treatment of depression during childhood and adolescents: Cognitive-behavioral procedures for the individual and family. In P. C. Kendall (Ed.), *Child and adolescent therapy: Cognitive-behavioral procedures* (pp. 165–208). New York: Guilford Press.

Taylor, J., Lindsay, W., & Willner, P. (2008). CBT for people with intellectual disabilities: Emerging evidence, cognitive ability and IQ effects. *Behavioural and Cognitive Psychotherapy, 36,* 723–733.

Thomas, E. J., & Ager, R. D. (1993). Unilateral family therapy with spouses of uncooperative alcohol abusers. In T. J. O'Farrell (Ed.), *Treating alcohol problems: Marital and family interventions* (pp. 3–33). New York: Guilford Press.

Thomas, P. W., Thomas, S., Hillier, C., Galvin, K., & Baker, R. (2006). Psychological interventions for multiple sclerosis. *Cochrane Database of Systematic Reviews, 1.*

Turner, H. A., Finkelhor, D., & Ormrod, R. (2006). The effect of lifetime victimization on the mental health of children and adolescents. *Social Science & Medicine, 62*(1), 13–27.

U.S. Department of Health and Human Services. (2001). *Mental Health: Culture, Race, and Ethnicity—A Supplement to Mental Health: A Report of the Surgeon General.* Rockville, MD: U.S. Department of Health and Human Services, Substance Abuse and Mental Health Services Administration, Center for Mental Health Services.

Wachs, T. D. (2000). *Necessary but not sufficient: The respective roles of single and multiple influences on individual development.* Washington, DC: American Psychological Association.

Wakefield, J. C., Kirk, S. A., Hsieh, D. K., & Pottick, K. J. (1999). Disorder attribution and clinical judgment in the assessment of adolescent antisocial behavior. *Social Work Research, 23*(4), 227–238.

Wampold, B. E. (2010). The research evidence for common factors models: A historically situated perspective. In B. L. Duncan, S. D. Miller, B. E. Wampold, M. A. Hubble (Eds.), *The heart and soul of change: Delivering what works in therapy* (2nd ed., pp. 49–81). Washington, DC: American Psychological Association.

Wampold, B. E., Mondin, G. W., Moody, M., Stich, F., Benson, K., & Ahn, H. N. (1997). A meta-analysis of outcome studies comparing bona fide psychotherapies: Empirically, "all must have prizes." *Psychological Bulletin, 122*(3), 203.

Watanabe, N., Hunot, V., Omori, I. M., Churchill, R., & Furukawa, T. A. (2007). Psychotherapy for depression among children and adolescents: A systematic review. *Acta Psychiatrica Scandinavica, 116*(2), 84–95.

Watson, J. B. (1930). *Behaviorism* (Revised ed.). Chicago: University of Chicago Press.

Webster-Stratton, C. (2012). *The incredible years.* Seattle: The Incredible Years.

Webster-Stratton, C., & Herbert, M. (1993). What really happens in parent training? *Behavior Modification, 17*(4), 407–456.

Weiner, B. (1985). *Human motivation.* New York: Springer-Verlag.

Weissman, M. M., Verdeli, H., Gameroff, M. J., Bledsoe, S. E., Betts, K., Mufson, L., ... Wickramaratne, P. (2006). National survey of psychotherapy training in psychiatry, psychology, and social work. *Archives of General Psychiatry, 63*(8), 925–934.

Weissman, M., Wickramaratne, P., Nomura, Y., Warner, V., Pilowsky, D., & Verdeli, H. (2006). Offspring of depressed parents: 20 years later. *American Journal of Psychiatry, 163*(6), 1001–1008.

Werner, E. E., & Smith, R. S. (2001). *Journeys from childhood to midlife: Risk, resilience and recovery.* Ithaca, NY: Cornell University Press.

White, C., & Barrowclough, C. (1998). Depressed and non-depressed mothers with problematic preschoolers: Attributions for child behaviours. *British Journal of Clinical Psychology*, 37(4), 385–398.

Wilson, G. T. (2013). Behavior therapy. In R. J. Corsini & D. Wedding (Eds.), *Current psychotherapies* (6th ed., pp. 205–240). Itasca, IL: F. E. Peacock.

Wilson, S. J., & Lipsey, M. W. (2006). *The Effects of School-based Social Information Processing Interventions on Aggressive Behavior: Part 1: Universal Programs*. Campbell Collaboration.

Wilson, S. J., & Lipsey, M. W. (2006). The effectiveness of school-based violence prevention programs for reducing disruptive and aggressive behavior: A meta-analysis. *International journal on violence and schools*, 1, 38–50.

Wolpe, J. (1958). *Psychotherapy by reciprocal inhibition*. Stanford, CA: Stanford University Press.

Wolpe, J. (1969). *The practice of behavior therapy*. New York: Pergamon Press.

Young, J. E. (1999). *Cognitive therapy for personality disorders: A schema-focused approach* (3rd ed.). Sarasota, FL: Professional Resource Press.

Young, J. E., Klosko, J. S., & Weishaar, M. E. (2003). *Schema therapy: A practitioner's guide*. New York: Guilford.

Young, J. E., Rygh, J. L., Weinberger, A. D., & Beck, A. T. (2008). Cognitive therapy for depression. In D. H. Barlow (Ed.). *Clinical Handbook of Psychological Disorders, Fourth Edition: A Step-by-Step Treatment Manual* (pp. 250–305). NY: Guilford Press.

Young, J. E., Weinberger, A. D., & Beck, A. T. (2001). Cognitive therapy for depression. In D. H. Barlow (Ed.), *Clinical handbook of psychological disorders: A step-by-step treatment manual* (3rd ed.) (pp. 264–308). New York: Guilford Press.

Ziegler, P., & Hiller, T. (2001). *Recreating partnership*. New York: W. W. Norton & Sons.

INDEX

CPSIA information can be obtained
at www.ICGtesting.com
Printed in the USA
BVHW010307260919
559422BV00002B/9/P

9 780199 937158